On the Edic

or

Survival after Death Scientifically Explained

by

ARTHUR FINDLAY

"Seek and you will find, for you have aids from
nature for the discovery of truth. But if you are
not able yourself, by going along those ways, to
discover that which follows, listen to those who
have made the enquiry." — *Epictetus*

PN PUBLISHING
THE COACH HOUSE, STANSTED HALL
STANSTED, ESSEX CM24 8UD

71st impression 2004
First published 1931

Published by
PN Publishing
The Coach House
Stansted Hall
Stansted
Essex CM24 8UD

ISBN 1 900671 02 6

THE SPIRITUALISTS' NATIONAL UNION was left
the copyright to Arthur Findlay's books with the request
to keep the them in print. The other titles available from
PN Publishing are:

THE ROCK OF TRUTH
THE UNFOLDING UNIVERSE
THE TORCH OF KNOWLEDGE
THE PSYCHIC STREAM
THE CURSE OF IGNORANCE Vol. 1
THE CURSE OF IGNORANCE Vol. 2
WHERE TWO WORLDS MEET
THE WAY OF LIFE
LOOKING BACK

Reprinted in England by Booksprint

CONTENTS

FOREWORD

In September 1924 I had printed a small book to which I gave the name *An Investigation of Psychic Phenomena.* This book contained a summary from my notes of my experiences with Mr. John C. Sloan, but it was printed only for private circulation.

It, however, only contained some of my experiences which I had originally put together for an address I gave to the Members of the Glasgow Society for Psychical Research on 25th March 1924. The same address was given to the Members of the London Spiritualist Alliance in the following month, and was afterwards published in *Light* between 19th April and 10th May 1924. I have also delivered this address in other parts of the country to large and interested audiences.

At the request of a number of those who were regular attenders at Mr. Sloan's séances I commenced the preparation of a larger book, to contain a more exhaustive account of my experiences with this gifted medium, but one thing and another has delayed its publication. I came to live in England, and had many interests to attend to, so that its completion was postponed.

It is, however, now completed, and the delay I am sure will not invalidate its contents. This book contains a faithful record of what I experienced on the dates given, taken from notes recorded at the time. Nothing has happened since then to alter my belief that I was privileged to experience phenomena super-normal in character and of comparatively infrequent occurrence. That these phenomena do occur, and that I actually was in touch with those who once lived on earth, and were known by the names they gave, I have not the least doubt.

ARTHUR FINDLAY.

Stansted Hall, Essex.
September 1931.

FOREWORD TO THE 29TH IMPRESSION

This book has now been before the public for just over three years. To me it is extremely gratifying that it has received such a warm welcome.

I have received thousands of letters from readers all over the world. The information given has confirmed some in their beliefs; while to others it has explained in scientific terms phenomena which they have experienced and could not relate to known laws. It has made it possible for others to accept the reality of psychic phenomena, now that these can be related to our present-day knowledge. Lastly, it is gratifying to know that the book has given comfort to many thousands by making them realise that death is but a door, the opening of pinions to fly, and not the closing of wings for ever.

I have nothing to withdraw from what I have written in this book. I have had much to add, and this is contained in the companion volumes which have followed, namely, *The Rock of Truth* and *The Unfolding Universe*. These three books form a Trilogy on Spiritualism which embraces the whole subject from every angle, and they are intended to lay the foundation for Spiritualism becoming accepted as the religion, the science, and the philosophy of mankind.

Professor Ernesto Bozzano, in his preface to the Italian Edition of this book, remarks that I have made no reference to what he terms "a luminous pillar which approaches Sloan, the medium, and is then absorbed by him," and he quotes the following extract from an article by Mrs. Hewat McKenzie, the well-known psychical researcher, published in *Light* in 1931, following the publication of this book:

"Mr. Findlay often mentions 'Whitey', the personal Indian Guide of the medium, and his valuable work in shepherding the spirits who came to make themselves known. I wonder if he saw, as I and others did, the coming and going of 'Whitey' as he took or relinquished control of his medium. He manifested his presence by a bluish clear light which could be seen approaching the medium as he sat playing at the organ before he fell into trance. It approached from his left, and came into view two or three feet away from him. As it reached him it was lost to sight. A grunt from Sloan would follow; 'Whitey' had taken possession of his medium, who stopped playing on the instrument, rose from the organ and took his place in the circle, being controlled by sitters on either side.

"I have often noticed the light approaching and said to myself, 'Whitey is here', and incidently heaved a sigh of relief that all would be well with the circle. My registration was correct in that always a second later Sloan was fully in trance. At the close of the séance 'Whitey's' light left the medium in the same way floating away into invisibility, and Sloan was his conscious self again. J. Malcolm Bird, of the American Psychical Research Society, sat with Sloan at the British College of Psychic Science, and in his book, *My Psychic Adventure*, describes 'Whitey's' light as from 6 to 8 inches across, flat and semi-circular. It rose diagonally from the medium's head and floated off and up. For a second or two it retained its original brilliance and then faded fast out of sight."

I have referred, in Chapter V, to the luminous lights which moved about the room during the séance, but I omitted to refer to this bluish light which came and settled on Sloan's head just before he went into trance, and left him just as he came out of trance. I, and all present, have seen it on many occasions, and I am glad my attention has been drawn to this omission, as it enables me to record that I likewise have seen the phenomenon. In whatever way it may be explained, one thing is certain, that it came and went with unfailing regularity, and corresponded with Sloan's entering and coming out of trance.

A. F.

November 1934

FOREWORD TO THE 38TH IMPRESSION

I have nothing new to add to what is contained in this book, except that I am now in possession of infra-red photographs which confirm, in all essential details, what I have been told by my communicators from the etheric world about the methods they adopt to enable them to speak to us on earth, by what we call the Direct Voice.

A. F.

October 1942

FOREWORD TO THE 41ST IMPRESSION

This book has been so often reprinted that the original type became quite worn out. Consequently the book has been reset for this impression, and I have taken the opportunity to have the letterpress thoroughly revised. A few additions were made, but nothing important was altered or withdrawn.

Since the book was written Sir Oliver Lodge, Edward C. Randall and Dr. John Lamond have passed on, but I have allowed the original text to stand on pages 25, 26 and 27.

A. F.

June 1945

VISIBLE AND INVISIBLE VIBRATIONS

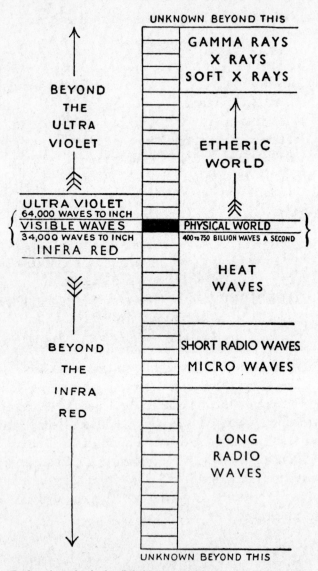

UNKNOWN BEYOND THIS

GAMMA RAYS
X RAYS
SOFT X RAYS

BEYOND
THE
ULTRA
VIOLET

ETHERIC
WORLD

ULTRA VIOLET
64,000 WAVES TO INCH

VISIBLE WAVES
34,000 WAVES TO INCH

INFRA RED

PHYSICAL WORLD
400 to 750 BILLION WAVES A SECOND

HEAT
WAVES

BEYOND
THE
INFRA
RED

SHORT RADIO WAVES
MICRO WAVES

LONG
RADIO
WAVES

UNKNOWN BEYOND THIS

The above chart makes clear how limited are our sense perceptions. Only the black portion represents the visible spectrum. This is all we sense of the innumerable etheric waves making up the Universe. The author has been told by his informants in the Etheric World that its vibrations just about touch those of the Physical World, and at times they can be detected by clairvoyance, by the seeing of etheric beings, called ghosts, and by psychic photography. Etheric waves, however, seem to be different from physical waves as so far we have discovered no instrument to contact them.

CHAPTER I

INTRODUCTION

"If any man can convince me that I do not think aright, gladly will I change for I search after truth, by which man never yet was harmed."—
MARCUS AURELIUS.

I HAVE thought much and pondered long over the strange experiences I have had during the last twelve years, experiences so strange, so foreign to all our accepted order of the phenomena of nature, that I can readily understand the difficulty many must have in accepting my records as true and accurate accounts of what really took place. I can expect only those who have had similar experiences themselves, to accept what I am about to tell without question or doubt. I know that if thirteen years ago I myself had been asked to believe these strange accounts I should have found it impossible to do so, but then my mental development was not sufficiently advanced to enable me to comprehend the subject. I then did not understand that these psychical manifestations, which it has been my privilege to experience, are like the other manifestations of nature, ruled by law and governed by order, and it is only when our knowledge advances sufficiently that this new science is found to harmonise with all that is already known.

As I say, I have had strange and wonderful experiences, because I have been brought into contact with a new world, a world which even the greatest thinkers on the subject are only now beginning to comprehend. My position has been a peculiarly privileged one, as twelve years ago I had the good fortune to meet Mr. John C. Sloan, one of the most gifted mediums in this country, and in his presence, when the conditions were suitable, voices quite extraneous to the medium spoke to me, claiming to be those of friends who, in my ignorance, I had looked upon as dead. These voices are not produced by the medium, and they occur, not only when others are present, but also when he and I are alone together.

They are not produced by any means of trickery, and I have come, after years of thought, to believe that those we call dead live on as men and women in a duplicate etheric body, and are able to manifest their presence again in this material world of ours, by borrowing from the medium a certain excretion, which emanates from his body. This enables them, for the time being, to materialise their vocal organs and thus vibrate our atmosphere.

We must first of all clearly understand that the etheric world is part of this world. That it is all about us. That it is material, though of a substance too fine for our senses normally to appreciate; that here and now we are etheric beings clothed in a physical body, and that death only means a separation of this etheric body from the physical covering. The etheric body is the real and enduring body, an exact duplicate of its physical counterpart. When this is appreciated it can be more readily understood how, under certain conditions which we do not yet fully understand, it can again clothe itself in physical matter, and behave under the control of mind in a manner similar to ourselves. So long as the thought prevails that the spirit of man is something of the nature of a puff of wind or a fleecy cloud, of no form or substance, so long will incredulity last among those who believe that all that is can be seen and heard, and that nothing exists outside the range of the physical world.

To enable those who once lived in this physical world of ours to re-materialise their bodies, composed of this finer etheric substance, certain conditions are necessary. The first is the presence of someone possessing a superfluity of the substance which of recent years has been termed ectoplasm or teleplasm. Whichever word will be ultimately adopted is a matter of no special importance. This individual is termed a medium, though it is believed that most of us have this quality of mediumship in a more or less degree, as we all have this substance within our own bodies. The recognised medium is different from us solely because he or she has this substance to a greater degree than the average individual, and it is thus more easily borrowed by the other world men and women who make use of him or her for the time being. In the case of the "Direct Voice", to which I am now referring, the best results take place in darkness, as light vibrations make it more difficult for this ectoplasm to be built up with sufficient solidity to vibrate the atmosphere.

Therefore, though I have heard voices in daylight, yet they are stronger and better developed in the dark or in a red light which has not the same destructive effect as white light. Quiet and harmonious conditions are also essential, and the condition of the atmosphere at times interferes with the results. For example, when the air is heavily charged with electricity the results are poor, the best manifestations occurring on clear crisp moonlight nights when the atmosphere is not too loaded with moisture. At the best the conditions making speech possible are very delicate, and only by experience can the best results be obtained, but when these do prevail the manifestations are indeed very wonderful. Voices of all degrees of culture and intonation address the sitter, and their peculiar tones can again be recognised as those pertaining to the individual when living on earth. The scepticism of the sitter may prevail for a time, but, if his honest desire for truth takes the first place, conviction is inevitable if the enquiry be pursued.

The object of this introduction is, in the first place, to clear away certain prejudices and misconceptions; in the second place to emphasise our colossal ignorance of the Universe; and in the third place to stress the great limitations of our sense organs. We should approach this new revelation with minds sufficiently plastic to enable us to readjust our views, and put aside any preconceived ideas we may have of what is possible and what is impossible.

Before going further, however, let me look back. The history of the Christian Church is typical of all movements either religious or political. Those in authority pronounced their dicta and those not in authority had to obey them. It was not in the interests of these rulers to improve the learning or relieve the ignorance of the people, and the people were so ignorant that they could do nothing more than obey those in power. That time is now looked upon as the dark ages, but, with the invention of printing, light began to shine into darkness. Then men's minds began to grow and to think. In 1543 Copernicus published his discoveries, and from that date a new outlook began to spread over Europe. We began to comprehend our relationship to the rest of the universe. Then came Kepler, to be followed by Galileo, Leonardo Da Vinci, Bruno, Newton, Darwin, and many others who carried forward the torch of learning and helped to dispel the ignorance of their times. They were denounced, excommunicated and traduced, but still they held to the path of truth, and now we find to-day every intelligent person accepting their views.

It was about the beginning of the present century that a change began to come over scientific thought, in the direction of viewing man not only as a physical but also as a spiritual or psychical being. This was caused by the discovery of the composition of matter, and by the gradual acceptance of psychic phenomena. Matter in the nineteenth century was looked upon as composed of atoms, little minute lumps of matter which congregated together to make big or little lumps as the case might be, just as a rice pudding is made up of various particles of rice. The discovery of the X-Ray brought about a further examination as to the constitution of things we see, and has resulted in the extraordinary discovery that matter is made up of what are called electrons and protons. These are not substances, as we understand the word. They are so minute that it is impossible to get down to them, and in consequence the nature and constitution of matter is only a question of inference.

What, then, is the material universe composed of? We really do not know, but there is one thing that scientific thought has begun to comprehend, and that is that the real universe is not the physical universe. In the days before Copernicus, it was thought that the sun, like the moon, circled round the earth, that the stars were points of light hanging from a huge dome, and their size was quite unrealised. The author of Genesis described their creation in six words as a kind of afterthought, "and he made the stars also". This earth was thought to be the centre of the universe; it was considered to be flat, and that space was empty except for the sun, moon and stars. That is how a child would describe the earth and the universe to-day, and that is how our ancestors described them four hundred years ago.

We are to-day in a somewhat similar transitory period. The average individual would say that what he saw, namely, the earth and all that composes the earth, was real and solid; that the sun was a real and solid mass, and that space was empty except for the stars and planets. That, most of us would say, is a common-sense way of dealing with such a question. What we see and handle is real, what we cannot see and handle is unreal. But just as the earth revolves round the sun and not the sun round the earth, so we are being led by science to look on the universe as something completely different from what it appears, and to regard a world unseen as also real, and what is seen as only real to us inhabiting physical bodies.

Let me give an example of what I mean. Supposing we were sitting in a church in the dark, never having seen the church, and could see only various glow lights moving slowly in innumerable different directions, everyone would say that the only things real in the church were the lights we saw moving about. That is our position in the universe to-day. These lights represent the stars, the material universe, but, when the church is bathed in sunlight, the lights we saw are made invisible by the daylight which reveals to us an entirely different aspect. When we are sitting in the dark and look at the points of light moving about, it is the same as looking at the universe with material eyes. When we sit in the dark we think that is all there is in the church, and that there cannot possibly be anything more, but when the daylight comes we see the pulpit, pews, windows and walls; in fact it is an entirely different view which we behold.

If two people were writing on what they saw, one during the time of darkness and the other in daylight, they would each give an absolutely different description, and yet it would be the same church and everything would be in the same place. We, in our physical bodies, are looking at the universe from the point of view of people in the church during the time of darkness. That is why a material explanation of the universe, based on the arguments put forward by materialists, is unwise, as they are looking at and considering only the physical universe, whereas the real universe is the etheric, and physical matter is but an intrusion in what we call space where the real universe exists. Space is the real universe. We think it is empty, but it is full of life and growth, a real objective world to its inhabitants. It is when we die and discard our physical body, that we look on the universe from the point of view of the people sitting in the church during the daytime.

The human being is composed of body, soul and spirit. The body is what we see, the soul is our mind, and the spirit is our etheric body which is an exact duplicate of our physical body. The etheric body holds our physical body together, and death is only the parting of the etheric body from the material body. This etheric body carries the mind or soul with it, and then we do not look on the universe from the material standpoint but from the etheric stand point. The material world becomes of no account, and the etheric world, what we call space, is the only one that counts. From what we know of its constitution it is permanent, while the material universe is constantly changing and decaying. No trace of decay can be found in this etheric universe; everything is constant and regular.

The mind of man is something super-etheric, a plastic substance which no one in the physical body is able to explain, but it must be super-etheric because it functions, guides and controls the etheric body after death. If it were not super-etheric it could be damaged or destroyed by those evilly disposed in the Etheric World. They can see the images it forms in our forehead; but they cannot touch it nor harm it. Except that they can see it working it is completely beyond their reach.

The etheric body is the body which holds together the material body on earth, and there is probably an etheric body for every living thing. The mind does not change by death, but only functions in different surroundings. The result is that it is only character and memory which really count, and the reason for continuing to develop our character must receive an impetus when it is known that as we develop here so shall we be hereafter. *but making further progress.*

Life is something quite apart from physical matter as it appertains to the etheric world. Why or when it entered into conjunction with physical matter we do not know, but there was a time far back in history when a living organism appeared. Then it was that life and thought in the most minute form took birth, and from it has evolved the complicated system of the human body and of all living things. We also do not know when this life was able to retain individuality; all we know is the fact that, so far as human beings are concerned, it can now function apart from the material body.

The material world is a transitory and passing world, and matter as we see it is the least important thing in the universe, though to us to-day it seems to be the most important. The things which are unseen are eternal; those things which are seen are temporal.

The nineteenth century added more to our knowledge of the physical universe than all the previous centuries combined. To-day knowledge grows so fast that the mind becomes incapable of assimilating more, and we sometimes think that we have reached the ultimate in what we can learn. The nineteenth century scientists dealt only with physical matter, and so we came to think that only physical matter existed. Knowledge advances by stages, and each stage is the foundation for the next. The foundation of physical science has certainly been well and truly laid, and the same law and order is found to exist wherever there is physical matter.

Physical matter, until comparatively recent times, was considered to be solid, and individuals were believed by Haeckel and Huxley, and the majority of nineteenth-century scientists, to be only physical productions whose thoughts and actions were produced in a purely mechanical manner. Just as there was no room for anything outside the physical world, so there was no place for anything apart from the physical body. All was solid matter, capable of being seen, touched and heard, and subject to certain well understood, immutable laws which governed the universe. In the slow order of evolution it was doubtless wise that this foundation to our knowledge should be so carefully laid, but we were in error in thinking that we had reached the bounds of knowledge and that nothing existed outside our physical senses.

Religion and science in those days were poles asunder, while the Church was able to keep within its folds only those whose faith exceeded their knowledge. Even theological creeds in time failed to hold the majority, and a blind fatalism settled on religion. The Church, no more than the scientist, knew anything of the after life, its Heaven was, as the well-known hymn told us, "far, far away", so far away indeed that the average thinking man ceased to believe in its existence. If he did, he had a nebulous notion of a new Jerusalem, painted in fantastic colours, the abode of the saved, and of an equally nebulous Hell, the abode of the damned.

Neither science nor religion knew that there existed around and about this world of ours another world of finer matter where those who died immediately entered, with an etheric body just as tangible and just as real as its physical covering which had returned to the earth from which it had come. Faith alone held aloft a dim and flickering light, prompted by some unerring instinct that death did not constitute the end of man, but that he was created to fill a larger part somewhere in the Great Beyond. Faith, however, received no help from science, which was looked upon by the faithful with dread and fear.

If science and religion both represent truth, such antagonism can be only temporary, born of ignorance on both sides. The dawn, however, is now breaking, and science is now leading us forward to a new day. It is becoming the partner of religion, and I can see the time coming, and coming quickly too, when science and religion will go hand-in-hand, brought together by the discoveries made by those who have devoted their lives to the furtherance of the knowledge gained by psychical research.

It is in the nature of man to press forward, and to peer further into the mystery of the universe. So the scientist has continued his search, and bit by bit he has found that the ultimate was further from his reach than ever, and that this physical world, which we consider so solid, is not so. Such a belief is one of the many delusions which we experience every day of our lives. The outlook of the twentieth-century man of science is vastly different from that of his predecessor of last century. First the atom was discovered, then the electron, and we are now asking ourselves if we have reached finality and if the electron is the ultimate basis of all substances.

In the last twenty years the unknown has widened and deepened; the Astronomer, on the one hand, with his telescope is penetrating further and further into space, and, on the other, the microscope is revealing new worlds which the physical eye unaided is unable to perceive. The physicists have broken up matter and now declare it to consist of various electrical charges. Its solidity has disappeared, it is found to be in constant rapid vibration, and the distance between the various electrons which constitute the atom is found to be, relatively, as great as the distance between the various planets which constitute our solar system.

Lastly, those engaged in the new science of Psychics are slowly but surely discovering a new world about and around us, one hitherto unsensed, but nevertheless very real. This etheric world, which is now becoming more and more a reality, is the subject of this book, and it is one which will command more and more attention as the years roll on. This new science, which to-day is the Cinderella of all the sciences, will in time take its place as the foremost and greatest of them all. We are on the threshold of a new age of thought.

The position which the science of Psychics has now reached is due to those pioneers of the past who laboured unceasingly in their researches into this hitherto unknown realm of thought. They braved the jeers and contempt of their fellow men, knowing that their labours rested on a sure and certain foundation. During the latter half of last century their discoveries received little attention, but, as the present century advanced, the hitherto incredulous and unbelieving public has been compelled, by the steady accumulation of facts, to modify its former hostile attitude. Consequently we find to-day, especially amongst the younger generation, a much more sympathetic attitude towards the subject.

To these early pioneers all honour is due. They were to be found in all sections of the community, though it was those men of outstanding eminence who suffered most from the abuse of an ignorant public. Amongst the earliest men of scientific eminence, Sir William Crookes and Alfred Russel Wallace will always be remembered for their courage and fortitude in proclaiming a new but unpopular truth. *Researches in the Phenomena of Spiritualism*, published by Crookes in 1874, will forever remain a monument to his honesty and courage.

Amongst other famous men of science, who were not ashamed to acknowledge their interest in Psychical Research, I would mention Lord Rayleigh, Sir Archibald Geikie, Sir J. J. Thompson, Professor Gilbert Murray, and Professor William James of Harvard. Another American, Dr. Hyslop, who devoted most of his later years to the subject, published his discoveries in several volumes which are of especial value owing to the careful manner in which his facts are recorded. In Europe, Lombroso and Flammarion, after years of study, declared their belief, not only in the phenomena, but also in an etheric world and communication between it and ourselves. Richet, the world-famous French physiologist, in his great work *Thirty Years of Psychical Research*, has accepted the phenomena though he still reserves his opinion as to their interpretation. He, however, already goes a long way on the road most enquirers have travelled, because a few years ago, writing in *Nature* on the subject of Psychic Science, he stated his opinion that

"Our intelligence is reached by forces that disclose facts which neither sight, hearing, nor touch could reveal."

This roll of men of science would, however, be incomplete if reference were not made to two of our greatest scientists who have identified themselves with the subject more than any of their contemporaries. I refer to Sir Oliver Lodge and Sir William Barrett, both of whom had the courage of their convictions in the early days, when belief in the reality of psychic phenomena was considered as a crime against all the tenets of orthodox science. I well remember the pleasure it was to Sir William Barrett to deliver a lecture on psychical research to an audience numbering thousands in the St. Andrew's Hall, Glasgow, some years ago. I had the honour to preside, and he mentioned to me, when he saw his audience, that forty years previously he had addressed the members of the British Association from the same platform on the importance of investigating the then little-known subject of Telepathy, but that he had received no support.

The whirligig of time, he aptly remarked, had brought about so complete a change that not only had he before him, on the present occasion, a large and sympathetic audience, and on the platform several university professors, but his subject embraced all the phenomena proclaimed as true by the Spiritualists forty years previously, and derided by the British Association of that day. Sir William was one of the founders of the Society for Psychical Research, and maintained his interest in it to the very last, as on the same day as he died he was present at one of its meetings. He was active and his mind was keen to the last. Every year that passed only strengthened his convictions, which will be found admirably expressed in his well-known book *On the Threshold of the Unseen*. Sir Oliver Lodge, fortunately, is still with us and loses no opportunity of proclaiming his beliefs. He may now be enjoying the satisfaction of having the intellectual world sitting at his feet, and accepting the results of his many years of research. I think, however, that he is too modest a man to find such enjoyment, though he would hardly be human if he, like Barrett, did not also feel that the whirligig of time is responsible for many changes, especially in the world of thought. (*See* Foreword to the 41st impression.)

In other walks of life, W. E. Gladstone must be remembered as having given his great name to the support of the Society for Psychical Research, and for many years before his death he was an honorary member. The Earl of Balfour, another eminent statesman, in 1893 was the Society's president. Bishop Boyd Carpenter, Archdeacon Colley, Sir E. Marshall Hall, Lord Tennyson, W. T. Stead; Watts and Leighton the painters, Ruskin, R. L. Stevenson and Andrew Lang, amongst the professions, occur to one, but the most outstanding of all, apart from the men of science, was undoubtedly Sir Arthur Conan Doyle, who probably did more to educate the public in the discoveries of psychical research than any other man. Mention must also be made of Sidgwick, Myers, and Gurney, whose disinterested courage and fairness did much to interest the more intellectual section of the public in psychic matters. The philosophic studies of Professor Henri Bergson, president of the Society for Psychical Research in 1913, have undoubtedly been largely influenced by his knowledge of the subject, and, lastly, reference should be made to Dr. Crawford of Belfast who did more than any other man to place the observed phenomena on a scientific basis, and in relation to the already known facts of scientific knowledge.

Psychical research is divided up into various sections. One, for instance, deals with telekinesis, or the movement of objects without physical contact, another with mental phenomena such as trance, clair-voyance, clairaudience and telepathy, while yet another is devoted to the study of what is called the Direct or Independent Voice. It is to this depart-ment of psychic knowledge that I have devoted much time and thought over the past twelve years, but there are others who have given much thought and study to its investigation and have reached the same conclusions as I have come to.

Vice-Admiral Usborne Moore devoted almost the entire part of his later life to the study of the Direct Voice, as it occurred in the presence of that famous medium Mrs. Wriedt, and his careful records will be found in his important book on the subject entitled *The Voices*. The special position he occupied in the Navy, with the necessity for the greatest care and accuracy, made him especially suitable for this research work, as his training had made him scrupulously accurate in all he undertook. Edward C. Randall of Buffalo, with whom I stayed when I was in America some years ago, has, however, been the most fortunate of all the investigators into this great sub-ject, as he experimented for over twenty years with one of the most highly-developed Direct Voice mediums, Mrs. Emily S. French.

This lady was under his careful observation during all these years, living much of the time in his own house in Buffalo. Investigations took place several times each week, and Randall, from open scepticism and disbelief, gradually, under the force of the evidence which accumulated, became convinced, as many others have done before and after, not only of the genuineness of the phenomena but also that the voices were produced by those who once lived here on earth. On over seven hundred nights, he told me, covering a period of twenty-two years, in his own house, under scientific conditions, he talked for hours on end with those the world thought dead. Randall is not a man to be easily convinced, or to be the subject of trickery. He is one of the leading lawyers in the United States, and besides that, he was, when I met him, president of several important industrial undertakings, one of which is the American Super Power Company, which supplies New York with electric light and power. This practical, level-headed lawyer, accustomed to the sifting of evidence and detection of fraud, has published the result of his investigations in several books, the principal of which is entitled *The Dead have Never Died.*

Those interested in the religious and philosophical side will find this well expressed in *Kathleen*, by my old friend the Rev. John Lamond, D.D., the biographer of Sir Arthur Conan Doyle, who, since 1878, has based his preaching on his wide experience of psychic phenomena. He is one of the pioneers amongst the clergy in his effort to bring orthodox religion into line with this new science. *Human Personality and its Survival of Bodily Death*, by F. W. H. Myers, in two volumes, and covering 700 pages in length, but now published in an abridged edition, was the outcome of a great scholar's life of research, and was the text book of the science at the beginning of this century. Much progress in understanding the laws governing the phenomena has, however, been made since its publication, but its carefully grouped records of cases in all the different departments of the science will for long stand as a monument of painstaking and careful research.

I have given a brief summary of some of the leading men interested in this great subject of the survival of death, but there are many others who have done much to further our knowledge on the subject. These men were the pioneers who have penetrated into the border-land of this newly-discovered country, and brought back to their fellow travellers towards this land they will all some day reach, many vital facts pertaining to their destination. The reports of the earlier pioneers were received with scorn and ridicule, but, undaunted, they insisted on the truth of their reports. Others went to seek this new found land and came back with the same news. So it went on, year after year, until at length unbelief gradually broke down, and the multitude then asked for more and still more information from the growing band of pioneers who had ventured on ahead.

One of the most recent and distinguished who has gone some further distance ahead of his contemporaries, and has had the courage to proclaim his discoveries, is Dr. R. J. Tillyard, F.R.S., Entomologist-in-Chief to the Commonwealth of Australia. He became convinced a few years ago of the reality of psychic phenomena, in consequence of certain investigations he made in this country and America. He was not slow to tell his fellow scientists that his discoveries had changed his outlook on life and the world in general, and that the sooner official science began a serious investigation into psychical phenomena the better it would be for science and the world at large. That his pronouncements made a considerable impression amongst the die-hards of the old materialistic school became quickly apparent, and, on the eve of his departure home to Australia, he had the satisfaction of hearing from the lips of Sir Richard Gregory, the Editor of *Nature*, words of great encouragement.

This occurred at a private luncheon given in his honour by the National Laboratory for Psychical Research, conducted by Harry Price, at which I was privileged to be present. Sir Richard, in the course of some highly appreciative references to Dr. Tillyard, spoke of him as having lighted a candle which had not yet been put out. I mention this incident so as to emphasise again that the pioneers have done their work well, and that official science and orthodox religion, where the worship of the past still reigns, are gradually, but nevertheless surely, moving in the direction in which psychic knowledge is leading them. Certainly the day is not far distant when those who deny the reality of psychic phenomena will be accounted foolish and ignorant.

Dr. Crandon, of 10 Lime Street, Boston, U.S.A., furnished me with the results of a private sitting held in Boston, at which the only person present was Dr. Tillyard. The medium was Dr. Crandon's wife, known to all psychic students as "Margery". I have not space at my disposal to go deeply into the pre-cautions taken to prevent fraud, and the results achieved, but one can say emphatically that everything possible was done to prevent the medium being responsible for what occurred. Dr. Tillyard was present with her in a locked room in the dark. Prior to the light being put out, and the door locked, the medium was securely fastened to her chair by means of adhesive tape bandages, the ends of which were marked by blue pencil, which blue markings were continued on to the medium's skin. If she had moved it would have been seen afterwards that the blue markings were out of place, but at the end of the séance they were in their correct place. It was physically impossible, therefore, for the medium to be responsible for what occurred.

During the séance, first of all thumb marks, whose markings did not resemble the thumb marks of either of the two present, were obtained on various pieces of soft wax, and later in the séance an indepen-dent voice, claiming to be the medium's brother, carried on an animated conversation with Dr. Tillyard. That it was independent and apart from the medium, and not her voice, was proved by the fact that during the time this voice was speaking the "Voice Cut-Out Machine" was attached to the medium's mouth. This machine is a device which has been invented to make it impossible for a medium, when it is in use, to speak. Therefore, when it is in use, if another voice speaks, it cannot be the medium's voice. Dr.

Tillyard's comments on this private sitting, which was held on 10th August 1928, are contained in a letter he wrote to Sir Oliver Lodge, dated 11th August 1928, of which the following are the most important items. They are taken from *Psychic Research*, the Journal of the American Society for Psychical Research.

"It seems to me quite impossible to find a single flaw in this wonderful result. . . . But my object is to record scientifically that they do occur, that they are part of the phenomena of Nature, and that Science, which is the search of Truth and for Knowledge, can only ignore them at the deadly peril of its own future existence as a guiding force for the world. This séance is, for me, the culminating point of all my psychical research. I can now say, if I so desire, *Nunc Dimittis*, and go on with my own legitimate entomological work. . . . I can only ask that you and your whole family will accept my statement as absolute truth, knowing me as you do. . . ."

To Dr. Crandon and his wife this remarkable testimony, by one who until a few years ago was a complete unbeliever, must be a source of great gratification, as, like all pioneers, Dr. and Mrs. Crandon have had to suffer the jeers of the ignorant. He, however, bravely risked his great reputation, believing that truth must ultimately conquer, and that to follow truth wherever it may lead is the only course an honest man can adopt. What happened in Dr. Tillyard's presence has happened in the presence of hundreds of people, who have experienced the same results with this lady. Consequently Dr. Tillyard's experience is only typical of many others, carried out with the same precautions and scientific care.

It is now possible to discuss psychic phenomena at a dinner table, at one's club, or in a railway train, without being made to feel that your friends look upon you with sincere pity as one so sensible in other ways, but somewhat unbalanced in this direction. I trust, therefore, that what I am about to relate will receive more consideration than was accorded to the writings of some who have gone before me. Evidence, cumulative evidence, and still more evidence will in the end win the day. With this weapon the walls of ignorance and antagonism are being brought low, and there is no stronger tool available to complete destruction than the evidence of survival obtained by the Direct or Independent Voice. Both names for this phenomenon are used, and they refer to the pheno-menon of voice production and speech from some intelligence quite apart from any being in the flesh.

The Direct Voice is the highest psychical pheno-menon yet discovered, and it is the most convincing besides being quite the most wonderful. All the other discoveries of man fade into insignificance when compared with this great discovery, the discovery of a direct method of communication between us and the departed, not by means of raps or taps, but by the most intimate of all forms of communication, the human voice. Other forms of psychic phenomena can be simulated by a fraudulent medium, but the Direct Voice at its best cannot be. Often have I, and others with me, heard two and sometimes three separate voices of different tone and personality speaking to those present at one and the same time, on different topics, known only to the person addressed, while the medium was either talking on some other subject to the person sitting next him, or I had my ear close up to his mouth and not a sound was proceeding from his lips.

From instances which I shall give, telepathy, cryptæsthesia, and the other explanations given by some to account for psychic phenomena, can be ruled out. A clear-cut issue lies before the enquirer, and I know of no one who has been privileged to experience the Direct Voice at its best, who has been able to come to any other conclusion than that the voices come from those who once lived here on earth, and who, having passed through death, now return to tell us that there is, in reality, no death but a fuller life of steady development and progression in an etheric world which interpenetrates this earth of ours.

In concluding this introduction to the subject I wish to say, with all the strength at my command, that there *is* continuity of life, that nothing is lost, and life is no exception. Communication between those now living in bodies covered with physical matter, and those who have discarded their physical bodies is not only possible, but takes place under suitable conditions. My results have been obtained by creating those conditions, conditions which made it possible for the discarnate to resume speech with the incarnate. It has been my privilege on many occasions to carry on conversations and discussions with those who have passed on to the fuller life, or to hear them carried on with those present along with me. Hundreds of different voices have I heard, and hundreds of facts have I and they been given, to prove that those who spoke were in reality those they claimed to be.

From these conversations I have learned much, not only of the continuance of life, but also of the conditions of life in this etheric world about and around us, and of the methods employed for communication. Much of what I was told I could not comprehend or understand, and, even after the devotion of much thought to the question over the past twelve years, I feel more than ever the profundity of it all.

Before, however, giving my records of some of these conversations, let me lead the reader on step by step, as a proper grasp of the subject can only be obtained by our having one foot securely placed on the first step before moving on to the next. The first step is a consideration of that little understood, but vastly important something, known to science as the Ether, which is believed to fill all space and is the medium of light, as well as of the sounds which come from our wireless transmitter. Until we understand a little of this invisible but very real thing, and how limited are our normal sense perceptions, it is useless even to attempt to get an intelligent understanding of the phenomena which occur in the séance room. This being so, my next chapter must be considered as a further introduction to the subject under discussion.

CHAPTER II

THE UNIVERSE OF ETHER

"The vast interplanetary and interstellar regions will no longer be regarded as waste places in the universe. . . . We shall find them to be already full of this wonderful medium; so full that no human power can remove it from the smallest portion of space, or produce the slightest flaw in its infinite continuity."—CLERK MAXWELL.

"Reality is what everyone is keen to know about. No one wants to be deceived; all are eager for trustworthy information, if it be forthcoming, about both the material and the spiritual worlds, which together seem to constitute the Universe. The Ether of Space is the connecting link. In the material world it is the fundamental, substantial reality. In the spiritual world the Realities of Existence are other and far higher; but still the Ether is made use of in ways which at present we can only surmise."—LODGE.

WE live and move and have our being in a physical world which is composed of substances vibrating within certain fixed limits, to which we give the name "matter". We are born into it, and we accept it as if it comprised everything. Yet how different things are from what they seem to be. Our ideas of the physical things about us change from age to age. Each generation imagines the absolute has been reached in knowledge, and yet history is just the story of the development of the human mind in relation to its surroundings. At no stage can it be said that the sum of human knowledge has been reached. One discovery is followed by another, and each time it is thought that the universe has no further secrets to yield up to man, that human enquiry has at last reached its limit. Then some new idea based on further knowledge is put forward, somewhat timidly to begin with, to be first scorned, then considered, and finally accepted.

So life has developed, mentally, from its primitive condition up to the present day. At every stage the mind has been able to take a larger grasp of its environment. To life, at its beginning, the sea in its immediate vicinity, through which it floated, was its universe, its all. That constituted all that could be grasped by the mind of palæozoic life. By slow, unsteady steps both body and mind developed, through the fish stage to the reptile, and so on, until the being we call man arrived. This creature, by developing his mind as well as his muscles, became in time the dominant power on earth. By a slow and painful path his development has proceeded, many of his failures and his mistakes he has remembered, most of the knowledge he has acquired he has not forgotten, and to-day he finds himself developed mentally and physically to a higher degree than ever before.

We have certainly found the means of controlling physical matter to a greater degree than ever before, but the question now comes as to whether this achievement is the goal of humanity? We now understand its laws and functions, but is this the end of human endeavour? As we were thinking that this was so there comes a new discovery. We are now told that just as our forefathers were wrong in their astronomy and had to re-cast their views, so must we re-adjust our ideas regarding this physical matter about which we thought we knew and understood so much.

Matter which looks so solid is in reality not solid at all. What we see when we look at a table or a chair, for instance, are the vibrations of a certain number of electrons, which are revolving at immense speed around a centre known as the nucleus. Matter is made up of atoms, and these atoms are in turn composed of electrons and protons. According to the number of electrons in an atom so is the substance, but the weight is conditioned by the number of protons. The number of planetary electrons in any element is given by its atomic number, but in addition to these there are electrons fixed in the nucleus, equivalent to the supplement of its atomic weight, and these are liable to vary in different isotopes.[1] The atomic number for iron is 26, while its atomic weight is a whole number somewhere about 56. Therefore, in iron there are always 26 planetary electrons, and in normal iron there are 30 in addition, though in some isotopes there may be 31 and in others 29.

Consequently, when we look at or handle something composed of the foregoing, we sense something to which we have given the name of iron, or, to put it correctly, when our eye is affected by the ether vibrations its electrons create, we create the mental image of iron. Our touch is likewise affected by the vibrations these electrons produce and they give us the effect of heat and cold, but the number of protons give us the sense of weight. Sir Oliver Lodge, in *Ether and Reality*, puts it as follows:

"We can now summarise briefly what we know. The two oppositely charged particles, the negative and the positive, are called respectively an electron and a proton. They are both exceedingly minute: and there is a sense in which their size has been

---

[1] ISOTOPE: Each of two or more elements—or atoms of an element—with identical chemical properties but different atomic weights.

measured. They are far smaller than atoms, incomparably smaller, the smallest things known: even if there were a hundred or a thousand of them in the atom, they would not be in the least crowded, there would be plenty of empty space. Different atoms are now known to be composed of a different number of electrons, and by their different number and grouping they constitute the different chemical elements. The atoms of all the chemical elements are built of electrons and protons and of nothing else. . . .

"On this view the existence of an electron can be fairly understood. Can the existence of a proton be understood too? No: there we are in a difficulty. The proton is more massive than can easily be accounted for: and why it is more massive we can only guess: indeed at present we can hardly guess, or at least the guesses are not very satisfactory. That remains at present an outstanding puzzle: the question is one that has hardly yet been faced. One guess is that the electron is hollow, like a bubble, that it has an electric field which by itself would cause the bubble to expand, but that it is kept in equilibrium and of a certain size by the etheric pressure. On this view there is no substance in its interior; in itself such an electron is not massive at all, its apparent mass is due to its electric field and to nothing else. Whereas the interior of a proton, instead of being hollow, may be full-filled with an extra ether, all that which was removed from the electron being crammed into the proton, so as to account for its great massiveness or what we may call its weight.

"A proton is more than a thousand times as heavy as an electron, about 1840 times by direct measurements; and what is called 'the atomic weight', or the weight of an atom, depends almost entirely on the weight of the protons it contains. The hydrogen atom contains only one, the helium atom contains four, the lithium atom seven, the oxygen atom sixteen and so on—in accordance with the list of atomic weights long empirically known in chemistry, the heaviest being uranium, which contains 238. The atomic weights are certain enough; the number of protons in a specified atom is fairly certain also. What is not known is why the proton has such a weight, and why the weight of an electron is so much less. In every other respect the two charges seem equal and opposite: electrically they are equal and opposite. . . .

"We are safe in saying that the weight of matter depends on the protons, that is the positive units, which go to form the nucleus of the atom, while the chemical properties of the atom depend on the electrons which circulate round the nucleus. These planetary electrons are active and energetic and produce conspicuous results: they characterise the atom by its spectrum; they confer on it its chemical properties; but they add to its weight hardly at all. It is a curious state of things, but the evidence for it, so far, is good."

Physical matter is in reality an open network of electrons and protons, and the distance between the electrons and the protons in an individual atom, in relation to its size, is immense. If we consider the nucleus as commanding the same position in an atom as the sun does in our solar system, then the relative distance the electrons are apart from one another and from the protons might be taken as equivalent to the distance the planets are from each other and from the sun. If we consider an atom as something the size of a village church, then a pin-head would represent the relative size of one of the electrons of which it is composed. These protons and electrons in the atoms are thus far asunder, moving at enormous speed, and they are linked together by this invisible ether which occupies much the greater space within the atom. Matter is thus constructed of minute electric charges, both positive and negative, not moving haphazardly, but freely and orderly, and connected together by the invisible ether, which is now believed to be the basic substance of the universe.

What then do we know of this invisible ether? We imagine it filling all space, though, as we cannot grasp space, we are unable to comprehend its extent. We know, however, that the ether waves can undulate through space at the rate of 186,000 miles a second, which undulations, or waves, give us what we term light. Under certain circumstances the vibrating energy of these waves of ether can be translated into equivalent energies of heat and electricity. Though we cannot see the ether yet we infer that such a substance exists, because heat, light and electricity travel through space at a definite rate, and therefore there must be a medium through which they undulate. Our physicists therefore argue that the ether is a pragmatic hypothesis, a logical postulate.

The ether has never been seen nor weighed as an actual substance, yet certain tentative conclusions have been come to concerning its character and properties. It fills all space, it is five hundred degrees colder than the temperature of the earth, it has inertia and momentum, it exercises pressure, and has density and elasticity and a perpetual squirming motion. Later experiments may modify this conception of this wonderful substance, which in itself we can neither see, hear, smell nor touch, and, when thrown into vibration, can carry across space the energy which is capable of entering our consciousness as light, heat and electricity. Only recently we have discovered how to transform these waves into words and music. This undulating substance is never at rest and is always in movement. Though it has never been seen nor touched, yet if it were non-existent we would be blind and cold, as there would be no medium to carry the waves which set up vibrations in our eyes and in our skins.

This amazing substance is the medium between things material and our senses, but matter is now considered to be this same ether in certain fixed states of vibration. The electrons in the atoms are particles of negative electricity and the protons are certainly electric in their nature. Both are etheric, and matter is only ether in a particular condition. All ether is potentially matter and all matter potentially ether. Physical matter, which appeals to our senses, is only that section of the ether which happens to be vibrating within certain fixed limits. In this book I differentiate between the two substances; physical matter on the one hand, which we can sense, and this etheric substance which is beyond our sense perceptions. Yet, though beyond our perception, it is not beyond our capacity to understand, at least in some degree. In fact, our understanding of it has increased so much in recent years that the whole tendency of physical science to-day is towards the view that not physical but this etheric substance is the basic structure of the universe.

The ether of space can now be taken as the one great unifying link between the world of matter and that which we term etheric, as it is the substance common to both worlds. Both are contained within this substance, both are part of it, and both are formed out of it. The two worlds are part of the same universe, and life in both is conditioned by it. Here, in this world of matter in which we function, we are only conscious of a lower scale of vibrations, whereas in the etheric world, where life also functions, consciousness is affected by a higher scale of vibrations. The ether is as much to other life in the universe as it is to us. To this other life its surroundings are just as substantial and real as ours are to us. Life functions in the ether, and it is just as much able to do so when free of matter as it is when clothed in matter; in fact, a fuller, larger life can be imagined when the physical body is discarded. As we proceed, these views will be better appreciated, as in my conversations with those in this further life, which I shall report, it will be seen that they tell me that the etheric world is just as real, just as tangible, just as beautiful, in fact more so, than the world of physical matter which appeals to our limited sense perceptions.

Only the ignorant affirm that just what we sense is real, that beyond this range of sense nothing exists. Our range of sense, our sight, our touch, our smell and hearing are limited to the last degree. We know that the spectrum of the spectroscope proves the very limited range of our ordinary vision, and that further ranges of vibrations of what would be colour, could we see them, extend on either side. It has been said that the perceived vibrations as compared with the unperceived are much less than is an inch to a mile. It is evident that there lies an enormous region for other life to inhabit around and within this world of ours, a region quite beyond our normal sense perceptions. (*See Chart facing Introduction*).

Until we clearly understand that our senses here only respond to a very limited range of vibrations, namely those we term physical matter, that outside these there is a universe full of life, which responds to a higher range of vibrations, unreal to us, but more real to it than physical matter, we cannot grasp or understand in all its fulness the psychical phenomena which develop through mediumship.

All my life these deeper problems of life and death have interested me. I remember at school passing a horse in a field and lying beside it was a dead foal, and I wondered then, as I have wondered often since, what had actually taken place to change what the day previous was an active moving piece of substance to one that was now inert and still. These thoughts have occurred to everyone from time to time, and they can be continued right through the entire range of living substances. What is the cause of a tree in full bloom retaining its shape and its leaves, while another which is called "dead", breaks in pieces at a touch and crumbles away into dust? There must be a something, to which we give the term life, which animates the living organism, and is absent in the dead organism. That something has the power to give the substance form and expression, whereas, when the something is absent, form and expression go, and the substance which was previously animated returns to form part of the earth.

It is, therefore, evident that there is something we cannot see or handle, and yet is real and powerful, which has this faculty of creating forms out of inanimate earth. I say it must be powerful, because it is capable of raising matter contrary to the force of gravity, and retaining matter in an erect position, as, when it leaves the substance, the force of gravity again assumes control and the substance in question is affected by all the forces of nature. A man, an animal, a tree, can stand erect when this life force permeates them, but when it does not they fall to the ground.

Life, therefore, is an organising force which can counteract the tendency in matter to disorganise itself. Life is a formative, thinking force, entering matter and arranging it, whereas matter without it is inert and devoid of personality. Life, therefore, cannot be a part of matter any more than the potter can be a part of the clay he uses in his moulds, and besides this it has personality. Every living thing has personality, as every living thing is different from every other living thing. This life force, by this process of arguing, has powers quite beyond the powers attributed to matter. It is more powerful than matter, it can organise matter, and therefore thinks. Besides that it has individuality. Consequently we can safely take a further step forward, and say that this organising force is influenced by mind and that this which we call mind must be the living, active, dominating, control-

ling force in the universe. Mind controls life and life
controls matter.

Death can therefore be described as a severance
of mind from its association with matter, and it would
be illogical to conclude that mind and its vehicle, the
etheric body, which have such power over matter,
cease to exist when we lose sight of their organising
powers. Though we do not see mind at work, it is
logical and reasonable to assume that it continues
to control this etheric substance elsewhere. Matter
we know can be changed, but never destroyed. Consequently it is safe to assume that what can control
matter likewise cannot be destroyed.

This general argument, had we not direct evidence,
might never lead us to anything tangible. We might
always be right in assuming the indestructibility of
mind, and its expression, life, but had psychic phenomena not come to our aid we would have been only
half-way to our goal. The goal, however, has now
been reached, and the path has been prepared for the
human mind to travel the whole road. Logically it
is a reasonable assumption that mind should continue to exist after death, apart from its association
with matter, but now we have the proof from psychic
science that this does so happen, and that the etheric
body which survives is the real body and the one which
holds the physical body together during life on earth.

Death, I am told, is as easy and as simple as going
to sleep and then awakening. Our etheric body slips
out of the physical body, carrying the mind with it,
and we awake to our new surroundings to find our
friends and relations ready to help and instruct us in
our new life. Death is simply the severance of this

etheric body, or structure, from the physical body. The physical body returns to earth, and the etheric body, controlled by the mind, continues to function in the etheric world which, though within and also without the physical, cannot be appreciated by us so long as we are inhabitants of the physical body. Our range of sight and touch is too confined for us to appreciate these finer vibrations.

Individuality therefore continues apart from physical matter, and we still think apart from the physical because the same mind which functioned, when associated with the physical body, now does so through the duplicate etheric body. We therefore continue to exist as separate thinking units in the etheric world, much as we do to-day, but with new surroundings. With the same capacity for expanding thought as we have here, our minds develop, and probably develop more rapidly apart from physical matter.

It will be seen from the conversations I have had with those who have passed on, that our etheric bodies are similar to our present bodies, and that is the logical conclusion when we admit what has been said before, namely that the etheric holds the physical particles together. This etheric body, moreover, has weight as well as form, as weight is only a question of degree. In the etheric world weight, which in the physical is determined by gravity, must be determined by some other force of a like nature.

We shall therefore have weight, form, individuality and the same mind then as we have now, but what of our surroundings? As to these, we can accept what we are told in these communications from the etheric world, as we can make certain logical deductions based on our physical surroundings. We are informed that the etheric world is similar to this world. Our world is composed of individuals, and other living things which are animated by a force we term life, controlled by mind. It is therefore not unreasonable to conclude that this force, combined with mind, which has the power to act on physical matter, and produce what we experience in the physical world, has the same power to influence etheric matter to produce trees, animals, and other living forms, similar to those we have in the physical world. Therefore it is not unreasonable to believe that the etheric world contains trees, animals and flowers, being to all intents and purposes similar to this world, and that when we make the change called death we shall find ourselves in a world very much like the one we live in to-day, except that we shall not be encumbered by physical matter. Consequently our mind will be more active, and our thoughts and movements quicker.

In this chapter I have tried to take the reader one step further forward. Reference is frequently made in later chapters to vibrations, and a general knowledge that the universe is nothing more nor less than ether in different states of vibration is essential if we are to understand the new world about which it is my intention to tell you. Until I was able to grasp the fact that here in this physical world of ours we sensed ether only at certain fixed rates of vibration, and that these were infinitesimal compared with its other vibrations, I could not comprehend the possibility of another world of life and form and feature about and around us. When we can come to realise our own limitations, we can then find room in our minds for something greater and beyond the boundaries set up by our limited physical sense organs.

About and around us, interpenetrating this physical world, there is another world into which we pass at death. It has been described to me by those who have spoken to me from it, but only in language suited to our finite minds. When asked how best to explain it to others I was told to compare it to a sea of ether, wherein personal movement is even more rapid and easy than that of a fish in water. Let us take, for example, the sea in which are floating sponges entirely submerged. Surrounding these sponges is a medium which supports life, and so the etheric world can be contrasted with water surrounding our earth, except for the difference that the sponge absorbs only some of the water whereas the etheric world is not only outside our earth but inside as well. Interpenetrates is the only word we have to describe something real inside something else which is real, and it is on the surface of this etheric world we shall some day live.

We are so made that in the physical body we are in harmony with physical surroundings. At death we leave our physical body and function in our etheric body. We pass into the new environment which surrounds us, an environment which supports life, just as water supports life. We on earth are in this sea of ether, though we know it not, and just as much now as we shall ever be. The difference death makes to us is not so much a change of location as a change of appreciation. We now only appreciate the physical, but then we shall appreciate the etheric. Only when we desire to do so shall we again get into touch with the physical, as the physical pertains to physical matter, and the etheric to etheric matter, each in its own order, the one difference being that they of the etheric world can come back to us at will, see us and appreciate us and our surroundings. We can but listen to what is told and try to imagine. We are like a blind person here on earth, as we cannot see these men and women of the etheric world, but conditions can be produced which enable us to hear them and from what we are told imagine as best we can.

I have been told by them that our greatest thinkers have not the least conception of the properties that make up the Universe. Our leaders of present-day thought, ignoring, as many of them do, the séance room and mediumship, are missing great opportunities for instruction. The orthodox thought of to-day holds the opinion that space is empty of other life. I say that it is not, but contains life and form and feature, because I have been told so by those who inhabit it, and surely they know more of their own country than we do. To refuse to examine the claims of psychic science, and receive instruction from those with greater knowledge and intelligence than we have, because the phenomena are contrary to what it is thought should be, is blind stupidity due to ignorance and prejudice.

CHAPTER III

MIND AND MATTER

"Whatever that be which thinks, understands, wills, and acts, it is something celestial and divine."—CICERO.

TO-DAY we can comprehend the Universe in a way as never before. It may now be legitimately assumed that it had no beginning and will have no end, that the universe reduced to reality is motion, of which the speed of light is the only absolute speed we know, as all other speeds are relative. To say that the universe is just motion and nothing more seems to be reducing reality to absurdity, so let me put it thus. The universe is made up of varying degrees of motion, some of which appeal to us physical beings and are termed physical matter, while there is much which goes past us making no appeal to our senses. Constant change must be going on throughout this vast region, with physical matter radiating itself into non-visible matter, if we use the word matter for the effect this motion has on mind. Mind is the highest range of vibration we know.

Those who look on the universe as made up only of physical matter, and nothing more, take the view that it is running down and some day physical matter will cease to exist. That, however, is a much too limited view. From my psychic experiences I prefer to consider physical matter as only part of the universe, and that just as the sun, for instance, is slowly radiating itself out of sight, so other worlds are forming by the slowing down of motion. Thus new physical worlds are gradually becoming visible to the physical eye. The universe is constantly changing, physical worlds, such as nebulæ, being slowly born to be seen by us physical people, whilst others like the sun are going back again to the substance from which they came.

It is so difficult to discuss a subject which resolves itself into motion, something so intangible, but matter is motion and motion is matter. Matter, therefore, is the universe, it makes up the universe, it is everywhere in the universe, there is no place anywhere where it is not, it never had a beginning, and it will never have an end. It is in constant movement, evolving or devolving from our point of view. There is no such thing as empty space. This matter, which in certain states of motion appeals to us as physical matter, in other states appeals to those in the etheric world, just as physical matter appeals to us. Consequently they have their tangible world on which things live and grow, just as we have ours.

How many different worlds or places of habitation there may be depends on mind. Without mind there is nothing, and only when mind is present is there any realisation of matter, physical or etheric. It might therefore be logical to say that where mind is not, then there is no matter, that the universe therefore can be reduced to this one something, to which we give the name Mind; but can we conceive mind without something to act upon? We only appreciate mind when acting on matter, so mind and matter, though different—one the active, the other the passive —must be co-related. The name we give to the substance which makes up the universe, namely Matter, must therefore include these active and passive states;

it must be dual in nature, as one without the other is impossible to imagine.

So mind and matter are thus linked together, and to think of the one without the other is impossible. Mind, this something which appreciates matter and can influence matter, is the dominant force or motion in the Universe. I must use the words force or motion, as I can find no others. Mind is as much a part of the universe as physical and etheric matter; it can have had no beginning, neither can it have an end; its property is its capacity to develop and enlarge thought, or, in other words, it has the capacity of forming itself into images seen or imagined and of causing movement. To us, mind is experienced in conjunction with physical matter, and, as this book proceeds, it will be found in conjunction with etheric matter as well, but what its history is who can tell? We doubtless only experience mind in a limited form, and what it has performed in the past, or is performing elsewhere beyond our ken, no human being can say.

Movement denotes mind. Is therefore all the motion which appeals to our senses, and to which we give the name matter, governed by mind? Where does the realm of mind begin? Does a stone contain a mind? Our physicists tell us that a stone is in a constant state of movement, electrons and protons in rapid orderly vibration. If it does contain, or is influenced by mind, it must be mind in its crudest and lowest form, but we should be unwise to rule out the suggestion. Certainly what constituted a stone can become the habitation of mind, as when by rain and frost it slowly becomes earth, it produces grass, which cows eat, to become milk, which builds bodies, which mind controls. We therefore cannot be dogmatic as to where mind is, or where it is not, though we may be on safe ground in accepting provisionally that where growth and development are there also is mind. When, therefore, we look about us we can see mind in all states of development, from the humblest fungus to the mind which controlled the hand which wrote the greatest tragedy ever written by man, *King Lear*.

We are only just discerning the real universe and its make-up, and the King of this unlimited region, namely Mind, is only just becoming dimly appreciated. Truly the search after the ultimate by humanity has been a long and broken one. Many indeed have been the byways traversed and the mistakes made before reaching to even our present-day assumptions; but these speculations have much to justify them, though it is unwise, without further knowledge, to press too far or too fast.

As the etheric universe becomes more and more revealed to us, so shall we be better prepared to grasp the universe more as a whole, and not look at it purely from the physical standpoint. This limited outlook will never explain the universe; time and space will for ever baffle us, and only by including the etheric, and mind, will the Riddle of the Universe ever be explained. Sir James Jeans, in *The Mysterious Universe*, remarks that "Mind no longer appears as an accidental intruder into the realm of matter; we are beginning to suspect that we ought rather to hail it as the creator and governor of the realm of matter."

Modern science is thus slowly moving towards what may be called the larger view of the universe, and in time the etheric will take the larger place, the physical shrinking into relative insignificance. All together, however, must be included to make up the true picture, and mind, with its capacity to construct, to think and to remember, must be given its rightful place as the all-governing power of the universe. "God is a spirit, infinite, eternal and unchangable" we are told in the Scottish Shorter Catechism. To-day, with our larger knowledge, we might say more correctly: Mind is infinite, eternal, always changing, always developing, always creating new forms from old and never at rest.

Physical and etheric matter, governed by mind, thus make up the universe, and so far as is known there is nothing beyond or above. Wherever mind is, there will be found physical or etheric matter, and so it becomes impossible to imagine a limited universe because it must be as unlimited as is mind, as mind cannot operate on nothing. Mind and matter must go together; no mind, then no matter. Consequently so long as, and wherever mind exists, there must also be matter, the universe being limited only by the bounds of mind.

Each one of us has his share of this universal mind, and its interaction with physical matter is evidently for the purpose of training it in mental image-making. Mind has the peculiar faculty of forming, or moulding itself into, the images and the movements of its surroundings. These it can reproduce at will, and, through the medium of physical matter, cause change and movement here on earth. In the etheric world it has the power of moulding etheric matter in a more direct fashion, and, by thought, surrounding etheric matter can be changed into the forms which the mind images.

Earth, then, is the training ground for mind which has become individualised. Here it is trained in image-making through contact with earth's grosser surroundings, and, as it develops, it takes more and more control over its surroundings. When it ceases to function through physical matter it takes greater and greater control of its surroundings in the etheric world, until ultimately we (as represented by our minds and our surroundings) become just as we think.

The individual mind of each of us, our ego or our self, is therefore trained in creative thought through contact with earth, which training conditions our surroundings here and hereafter. The mind evidently never dies, but continues developing for ever, and, with its increasing command over its surroundings, both space and time become of less and less account. My mind is "me" and your mind is "you". It has been in existence for all eternity, though not so individualised as now. When it starts its earth experience it enters on a road which enables it to mould its surroundings more and more as it thinks, and its destiny, my destiny and your destiny, the destiny of every individualised mind, is to become just as it thinks.

Our minds will ultimately be in complete control of our surroundings, and, as we think, so shall we be. This, I believe, is our destiny, and our first step towards reaching this control over our surroundings, over time and space, is our time on earth, it being to achieve this end that we, as individualised minds, pass through our earth experiences.

CHAPTER IV

THE MEDIUM

"An honest man's the noblest work of God."—POPE.

MR. JOHN C. SLOAN, in whose presence the experiences I have to relate occurred, is a middle-aged man of slight build and a quiet manner. He has rather a dreamy expression, and, when sitting still and not speaking or taking part in a conversation, he seems to lose touch with his surroundings. At these times his eyes take on a far-away look, and when spoken to he is palpably startled. He enjoys quite good health, and at his work few would notice certain peculiarities which become marked in his own house when his work is finished. When he has nothing special to occupy his attention this dreamy state seems to take hold of him, and he becomes absent-minded and forgetful. Except for this he is like any other healthy normal individual.

All his life he has been aware that supernormal occurrences took place in his immediate surroundings. In his youth he was often disturbed by rappings and strange voices which he could not understand, and, during the past thirty years, these have developed into manifestations of a general and varied nature. His mediumship during these years has embraced trance, telekinesis, apports, direct voice, materialisation, clairvoyance and clairaudience. These have varied in degree year by year, but his friends generally agree that fifteen years ago his mediumship was at its best.

To those who have had little experience of these phenomena, let me explain. Trance is a state of unconsciousness certain abnormal people experience. It might be compared to falling into a deep sleep with a short interval between consciousness and unconsciousness. It is, however, more than sleep, it is a much deeper state of unconsciousness, the personality is withdrawn to a greater extent, and the body is more insensible to pain. A person in trance can be better compared to one under an anæsthetic than to one in sleep, with this difference, that the trance state may last for from two to three hours, and be repeated several times a week, without any ill effect being noticeable.

When Sloan is in this state he speaks, but it would be more correct to say that his vocal organs vibrate the atmosphere, as no one can be with him long, while this is taking place, and think that his own personality is responsible for what is said. The voice is different and the accent is different, and much of what is said is quite outside his range of knowledge.

Clairaudience and Clairvoyance are the powers some have of hearing what to others is inaudible, and seeing what is normally unseen. Both are due to the etheric structure of the ear and eye functioning abnormally, and thus these organs can catch the etheric vibrations. Telekinesis is the word used for the movement of objects without the use of any known force. Apports are objects brought from one room to another, or from a distance to where the medium is, by some invisible agency.

What is called the Direct Voice is the special subject of this book. In the medium's presence, but quite apart from him, voices, claiming to be those of deceased people, speak, and, when replied to, answer back intelligently, which proves that there is not only a mind behind the voice but that the intelligence is able to hear as well as to speak. When first experiencing these phenomena I naturally thought that the medium was impersonating people, as, when these voices speak, it is generally in the dark, and what could be easier than that he should be tricking me and others into believing that we were speaking to our departed friends?

On the first occasion I experienced these voices I was decidedly suspicious, and yet, as the séance went on, I wondered how it would be possible for any man, even if he had accomplices, to carry on such an imposture for over three hours. Thirty separate voices spoke that night, of different tone and accent, they gave their names, their correct earth addresses, and spoke to the right people, who recognised them, and referred to intimate family affairs. Never once was a mistake made, and the darkness really increased the evidence in favour of the genuineness of the whole proceedings. Difficult as it would be to remember everyone's departed friends and relations, and their family affairs, in the light, it would be doubly so in the dark, because fifteen people were present and the medium would have to remember exactly where each one was sitting. The voice on every occasion spoke in front of the person who recognized the name, the earth address, and the details which were given.

It was all very mystifying, and the fact that sometimes two or three voices spoke at once did not make it less so. There must be accomplices, I thought, and not only that but a regular system of gathering information. How it could be done in so thorough a manner was the question, but yet, on the other hand, how could the dead speak? Even if they lived again their physical vocal organs were certainly buried, and how could the atmosphere be vibrated without a physical bodily instrument? No, nothing so impossible could happen. I had heard of frauds and impostors, but never of the dead speaking, so the balance was certainly in favour of fraud.

So ran my thoughts that memorable night of the 20th September 1918, when suddenly a voice spoke in front of me. I felt scared. A man sitting next to me said, "Someone wants to speak to you, friend," so I said "Yes, who are you?" "Your father, Robert Downie Findlay," the voice replied, and then went on to refer to something that only he and I and one other ever knew on earth, and that other, like my father, was some years dead. I was therefore the only living person with any knowledge of what the voice was referring to. That was extraordinary enough, but my surprise was heightened when, after my father had finished, another voice gave the name of David Kidston, the name of the other person who on earth knew about the subject, and he continued the conversation which my father had begun. No spy system, however thorough, no impersonation by the medium or by any accomplices could be responsible for this, and, moreover, I was an entire stranger to everyone present. I did not give my name when I entered the room, I knew no one in that room, and no one knew me or anything about me.

That was my first introduction to John C. Sloan

and the Direct Voice, and after the séance was over
I asked him if I could come back again, as I was
anxious to know more about this subject. "Certainly
any time you care to come I shall be pleased to see
you," was his reply, and I turned to someone standing
near and asked how much I should pay Mr. Sloan. I
have always remembered the reply. "If you suggest
such a thing as paying him he will be deeply offended;
he does this as a duty, not to make money out of his
mediumship." That did not impress me as the method
adopted by a fraud. How could a working man earning a few pounds a week, I wondered, afford the time
and the money to gather all the information I heard
given to the people present that evening? I was so
impressed with my strange experience that I went home
that night, and wrote till the small hours of the next
morning a careful account of all that occurred at this
my first séance, and this practice I have constantly
adopted unless I had a stenographer present.

Slowly, but steadily, I came to understand that
what I thought was impossible was really possible,
what I thought could not occur did occur, that those
I thought were dead were very much alive, that they
had bodies of finer texture but similar in form to our
own, and that the medium gave off a substance which
enabled them to materialise their etheric mouths and
throats and tongues and again vibrate our atmosphere.
Further, I learned that as physical life can only gather
round it matter, in the initial stage before birth, in
the dark, so darkness was required to enable materialisation to take place from the substance drawn from
the medium. This I learned only slowly and after
I had given much time and thought to the subject,

but before I tried to know how it was all accomplished
I set myself to prove the medium's honesty. This I
did in many ways, as will be mentioned as we proceed.

After that first night many friends who had died
spoke to me, giving their names and correct addresses
on earth, and told me things which no one present
except myself could have known. Then I thought it
might all be telepathy, though how telepathy could
vibrate the atmosphere as a voice, which I recognised,
I could not understand. However, I wished to leave no
stone unturned to get at the truth, and so I waited to
see how long this theory would hold the field. It was
not long till it, like the fraud theory, had also to go.
Friends came and spoke to me, and told me things
that not only no one present knew, but that I did not
know myself, and never had known. These things
I found on enquiry to be correct, so thought trans-
ference between my conscious or subconscious mind
and that of the medium was ultimately ruled out.

I next decided to take the first opportunity to sit
beside the medium, and when a voice was speaking
to put my ear right up to his mouth. I held his hands
from the beginning of the séance, and when a voice
spoke I put my ear close to his mouth. I felt his breath,
my ear and his lips were just touching, but not a sound
was to be heard. This I have done, not once or twice,
but many times, until finally I was convinced that the
phenomenon of the direct voice was not only genuine
but that those who spoke were those they said they
were, our friends and relations, who, though parted
from their physical garment, continue to live a life
much as we do here. When able to gather sufficient
ectoplasm from a human being, called by us a medium,

they can, by lowering their vibrations, vibrate our atmosphere, speak to us, and hear us when we reply.

After twelve years' intimate experience of Mr. John C. Sloan, and having sat with most of the other leading mediums in this country and America, I can say with conviction that he is the best Trance, Direct Voice, Clairvoyant and Clairaudient medium with whom I have ever sat. Though trance utterances never appeal to me as does the Direct Voice, yet his powers in this direction are remarkable. His power of hearing clairaudiently is extraordinary, especially his faculty of getting the names and addresses of those speaking, a task which most mediums find difficult to do.

If he had been willing to give his gifts to the public, he would have been known as one of this country's most famous mediums. Instead of this he has preferred having his friends to his house for an evening, once a week or so, and giving them the pleasure of meeting again those of their acquaintances who have passed beyond the veil. He is retiring to a degree and modest in the extreme. He cares nothing for the praise which so often comes at the end of such an evening. He always gives me the impression that he dislikes these séances and only holds them as a duty. I know that, if left to himself, he would never exercise his mediumistic faculties. His sense of duty and kindness of heart are the reasons why his friends have been so specially privileged.

I know no man more honourable, of kinder nature, or with more of the old Scottish type of independence. So long as he can get work he will never take money in exchange for his gift. He has had his ups and downs, and, though a good and trustworthy workman, he has been out of work occasionally through no fault of his own. On one occasion Mr. McCully (some of whose experiences are recorded in Chapter X), who was one of the regular attenders at his weekly séances, told me that when Mr. Sloan had been out of work for some time a proposal was made that he should take something from those who came, and that they would bring others also who would gladly pay. Very reluctantly he agreed to give three séances on these terms, but after the second he refused to give the last. "I have now got a job," was his reply, "and I shall never again take money for my mediumship, if I can get work to enable me to support my family." The third séance was, however, held only on the condition that no payment was made.

Such is John C. Sloan, quixotic, yes; stubborn, yes; but only in what to him is a matter of conscience. No one need ask him for permission to be present at a séance and fear refusal; no one need fear that he will be made to feel that a favour is being granted. To Sloan, his duty is to give his gift to those who need it, but no money need be offered, as it would not be accepted.

It may be considered extraordinary that a man with such gifts should be so little known, but this is entirely due to his modesty and retiring disposition. He hates publicity of any kind; he is so shy that on occasions, when I have asked him to give my own friends a sitting in the séance room at the offices of the Glasgow Society for Psychical Research, he has asked me not to introduce him, just to let him come in, take his seat, and then have the lights put out. He is at his ease only when in his own house, his own friends gathered round him, and the séance takes the form of a religious meeting, as to him it is a holy communion with the unseen. His reward, he says, is in sending away some sorrowing one with the knowledge that life continues beyond this world, and that he has been the means of bringing together a bereaved mother or widow and a son or husband who has passed into the beyond. To see their happiness, after he comes out of trance at the end of a séance, is to him ample reward for all his trouble. Hundreds upon hundreds have received this comfort and consolation through his instrumentality. He only claims to be an instrument; he says he knows nothing as to how it all comes about; he has read little on the subject, and, as he is in trance throughout the séance, he knows nothing of what takes place.

Had Sloan been made in a different mould, he could have made an easy living by his gift and become known as one of our most famous mediums, but he has been content to live simply by the labour of his hands, earning a few pounds a week. He has brought up a large family in a small, but comfortable house in one of the working-class districts of Glasgow, and often he has had a hard struggle to make ends meet. He performs his daily work conscientiously and well, and his employer, who often was present at his meetings, considered him one of his best and most trustworthy workmen.

Such is the man I met that evening, now over twelve years ago. I was then ushered into a small room, in which were gathered over a dozen people, and, after some preliminary conversation, we sat down in a circle, Sloan on the music-stool beside a small harmonium. The lights were put out, and the room

was in complete darkness. After a preliminary
prayer, Sloan turned round and played several hymns
in which we all joined, but before the last was finished
he became controlled by an entity who goes under the
picturesque name of "Whitefeather". He was usually
addressed by us as "Whitie", a most amusing personality, who says that when on earth he was a Red Indian
Chief, that he lived in the Rockies and consequently
thinks our Scottish scenery tame in comparison.

During the sitting Sloan, so far as I could judge,
remained seated on the stool. Voices of all degrees
of strength and culture spoke, from what appeared
to be all parts of the room, but it was difficult to say
where they actually originated, as in the centre of the
circle were two megaphones, or trumpets, each about
two and a half feet long, and from the metallic ring
of the voice it was evident that they were occasionally
being used to speak through. All the time the two
trumpets, when not being used to speak through,
went round the circle touching each one gently. Someone would be lightly touched on the point of the nose,
another on the top of the head, another's hand would
be touched, and so on—never a hard knock. At
request, any part of the body would be touched without a mistake, without any fumbling, a clean, gentle
touch, an impossible feat for any human being to do in
pitch darkness, as I have proved on various occasions.
At times they moved so fast over our heads that they
caused a swishing sound. Lights, about the size of half-
crowns, of a phosphorescent appearance, were moreover continually moving about the room at all angles.

Looking over my records I find that I have notes
of forty-three different séances at which either I or

my friends had conversations with those who claimed to have known us when on earth, thirty-nine of which have been with Sloan, four with other mediums. I have also witnessed, at different times, the same phenomena with the leading direct voice mediums, both in this country and in the United States, so I think I may claim to have sufficient experience to enable me critically to examine the phenomena and record my conclusions.

As I say, I have notes of thirty-nine different séances with Sloan; eighty-three separate voices have spoken to me, or to personal friends I have brought with me, and two hundred and eighty-two separate communications have been given to me or to them. One hundred and eighty of these I class "A1", as it was impossible for the medium or any other person present to have known the facts then given. One hundred I class as "A2", as by means of the newspaper or reference books the medium could have found them out. One item of information given me I have not had the opportunity of verifying, and only one I have found to be incorrect. This latter was right up to a point, but, as it was a message given me by a voice on behalf of another, it is possible it was wrongly delivered. If it had been delivered in a slightly altered form it would have been correct, so I think that this one exception need not invalidate in any way the other items I have had correctly given.

Within the last few years changes have occurred in Sloan's life. His daughters married, his sons went to sea, and he consequently found living alone monotonous. His wife's people were sea-faring folk, and his sons followed the same calling. He also had a longing all his life for the same life, and, as he had no ties to keep him on shore, he likewise followed his sons and joined an Atlantic liner as Master-at-Arms, a position which he held for some years when he decided to come and live again on shore. He is now employed with one of the leading business houses in Glasgow, but continues to give séances to his friends. Only occasionally, however, does he now exercise his gift of mediumship, as his health is not so good as it used to be.

As I have already said, it seems strange that a man of such exceptional gifts should, for all practical purposes, be unknown to the world, but so it is. It can only be attributed to his persistent refusal to accept money and become a public medium, and nothing will change him from this course. He writes to me at times and I hear of him through mutual friends, but we seldom meet now, as, living in England as I now do, I am only occasionally in Scotland. I have, however, my notes to remind me of the many interesting and instructive times I spent in his presence, and all my life I shall be grateful to him for the kindness and courtesy he has always shown me.

I look back on the night we first met, and feel that I was there in the position of one who was looking for something which lack of knowledge had prevented me from finding. That night he gave me the chance of discovering what I had been seeking, the proof positive that we still live beyond this narrow vale called life, and that, when the end of earth life comes, we not only enter a larger and fuller one but also join again those we once loved here. For this, my life-long gratitude will be felt towards John C. Sloan.

CHAPTER V

THE SÉANCE

"Science is bound by the everlasting law of honour to face fearlessly every problem which can fairly be presented to it."—KELVIN.

THE reader has now been introduced to the medium, so the next step forward is to describe what takes place at a séance. What parts do the medium and the sitters play? The medium, in this case, lives in a small but comfortable house near one of the busiest thoroughfares of the city, but quite far enough away to be clear of the noise of the ceaseless traffic. The door of his house leads the visitor into a passage, and on the left-hand side there is a bedroom and a kitchen. On the right-hand side is his sitting-room, where the séances are held.

Usually from ten to fifteen people gather on such occasions, but the arrangements are not made by the medium. He takes no part in arranging who are to be present. Mr. McCully, who holds a responsible position in a leading Glasgow business, took the responsibility of making up the gatherings. Those present varied week by week, and usually half the company were people who had come for the first time or had only been occasionally before. The nucleus of the circle only was composed of regular sitters, and these helped in the results because it will always be found that those who sit regularly are able to help by influencing the conditions. Harmony is the most essential condition necessary for a successful séance, and I have always found that the best results are obtained when those present are in sympathy with each other and when only good feeling exists. When people are present who dislike each other, or are flustered or in any way excited, the conditions are adversely affected.

For that reason it is unwise for a party of novices to gather together in the presence of a highly-developed medium, and expect good results for the first time. That is impossible, and for this reason it was always found wise to have as many regular visitors as possible to keep conditions good, and yet allow strangers to come and get the experience, or the comfort, such a séance gives. The regular sitters have passed through the doubting and sceptical stage, the stage that every thinking person goes through. They have had their own experiences of their friends' return. They maintain a placid attitude, and this helps to counteract any adverse influence produced by the strangers present.

Those who attend séances are always hearing about vibrations. Even outside the séance room we are becoming accustomed to think in terms of vibrations, and the discovery of wireless transmission has done more to educate the public on the question of vibrations than any other discovery made by man. We have already discussed the ether, and every thinking person knows that our radio set will not give such good results on some days as on others. However good the transmission may be, and however good our receiving set may be, it can be adversely affected by what are called oscillations. Now, the person who oscillates and annoys us in this manner, upsets our wireless conditions just as does the person who goes into a séance room hostile or angry. The ether plays an equally large part in the séance room as it does with our radio instrument.

It may seem strange to some when I say that our etheric body, which is an exact duplicate of our physical body, affects the ether surrounding it. Each one of us vibrates the ether in his or her own particular way. From the body of each one of us are emanating vibrations of a different degree. The vibrations of a man or woman in anger are different from those of a man or woman at peace. The vibrations of a person who enters the séance room in a definitely hostile attitude so affect the conditions that phenomena occur less easily.

I know that it is often thought and said by people who investigate in this spirit that they never get results, and then they think that these results cannot possibly occur with others. If such people would only realise that a critical and keenly active mind does not upset conditions, and that they are not expected, nor asked, to put their reason in their pocket when they enter the séance room. I personally have never done so. I am as keenly critical to-day as I ever was, and if anything occurred in the séance room of a suspicious nature I think I should be one of the first to notice it. Nevertheless I generally get extremely good evidence of a super-normal nature.

I prefer to treat the medium as I do any other person I meet. Because someone is a medium it does not follow that he is a rogue and a knave. I admit that amongst mediums, as amongst every other class, there are some who are disreputable. I have met dishonest mediums, just as I have met dishonest people in my business and social life. Would we trust our body to every man who says that he has the power to heal it? Certainly not. We use our reason and our discretion, and if we are foolish we shall probably suffer by letting our bodies be treated by someone who professes to be able to do something he has not the capacity to perform.

Likewise, when you meet a medium, treat him as you would treat any other person you meet. If it is a trance sitting you are having in the daylight, judge by what is said as to whether it is super-normal or not. Judge as to whether it is possible for him or her to have obtained the information normally or not, and weigh up the pros and cons in a judicial manner. When sitting in the dark séance room for direct voice phenomena, make certain that the medium is not himself speaking. Besides this weigh up the communications you receive, and find from them as to whether there is evidence of a personality apart from the medium, and of the personality who purports to be speaking.

This has been my plan throughout, keenly critical and yet never hostile, and so I have surrounded myself in consequence by what we term the best conditions. These are the conditions which surround the regular sitters at Sloan's séances. They emanate vibrations which make it possible for those on the other side to get through to us, even if there should be another person present who is hostile. If his "oscillation" is not too strong, the emanations from the other sitters are strong enough to counteract his adverse emanations, and satisfactory results follow.

Some people, however, even though they may not

be hostile, never get results, through no fault of their own. We meet people in daily life whom we instinctively dislike, we know not why. These people may be liked by others with perfect justification, but, so far as we are concerned, they rub us up the wrong way, so to speak. If we said they upset our vibrations it would be more correct. We are not harmonious as we do not get on together, and so it is that some people never get results because they emanate vibrations which make it impossible for those on the other side to get through to them. The vibrations of the two personalities clash and spoil the necessary conditions.

That is why some people are bad sitters and others are good sitters. The average person can get on with most people in daily life, but there are others who are always rubbing people up the wrong way, or being rubbed up the wrong way, by those they meet, and that is why some people are able to get into contact with these finer vibrations while others cannot do so. Probably the great majority are in a similar position to myself in this respect; in fact, judging by the communications I have heard pass between people at séances and those of the other world, by far the majority must be similar to myself.

We, however, cannot overlook the fact that there are certain individuals so constituted that they do not get on with other people here on earth, their vibrations being at variance, and so, when they go into a séance room, they repel any attempt made by the other-world people to get in touch with them. It must not be thought that I mean that the conditions are exactly similar, because they are not, as some of the nicest and most agreeable people find it impossible to get results. What I mean is that, with our earth experience of different people, it can be better understood how it is that some people may be good sitters and others may not be. Good sitters emanate vibrations which enable those attempting to communicate to get through their communications. The bad sitters emanate vibrations which make it impossible for this to occur. That is why it is eminently desirable to get people sitting together who emanate vibrations which do not clash one with the other. Harmony is the aim; harmony is as necessary as a powerful medium, and that is what we have always tried to cultivate at these Sloan sittings.

Nothing helps better to engender harmonious conditions than music. Musical vibrations, though they are carried by the atmosphere and not by the ether, have an indirect effect on the vibrations we send out into the ether, and so it is that we start our séances by singing, accompanied by the harmonium. Sloan prefers hymns to secular music, but this is not necessary. Any music has the desired effect, but at Sloan's séances hymns only are sung, and if conditions become tense, and voices become weak throughout the sitting, we sing again. This has generally the desired effect, namely the improving of the means of communication between the two sides.

After the people assemble and engage in a preliminary talk, we sit down in a circle, the medium being one of us; men and women as much as possible alternate, as here again conditions are helped by having the grosser and finer vibrations of the two sexes mixed. In the centre of the circle are placed two megaphones, which have already been described. Conversation is general and encouraged, as talking helps conditions. There is generally a preliminary prayer, then a hymn, but before the first hymn is finished the medium has often relapsed into silence, and his head gradually nods, just as if he were going to sleep. His right hand is taken hold of by the person sitting on his right side and his left hand by the person on his left. The light is put out and we all join hands, forming a chain, and sit like this throughout the proceedings.

The singing continues, and after the first hymn another is sung, but by the time the third is finished Sloan is in deep trance and we hear mutterings coming from his mouth. These mutterings gradually assume more detail and we hear words being formed, indistinctly at first, but gradually becoming more and more distinct and better heard. Then with a shout Whitefeather, the control, announces his presence: "Good evening, friends, Whitefeather here now, medium's spirit out of his body and me in control, me hear all right, me can make his mouth speak what me want to say. Good evening, everybody." Such is generally his salutation, and we all say. "Good evening, Whitie," and express our pleasure at hearing him speak again.

Usually the first question we ask him relates to the conditions, are they good or are they bad? Whitie is a pessimist of the deepest dye. I have been told that the pessimist is one who has always lived with an optimist, and I think that Whitie's friends must all be optimists because he invariably tells us that the conditions are bad and that nothing will happen.

We know, however, not to take this engaging personality too seriously, and we always try to take a brighter view and say that we are sure things will come all right. His pessimism is generally unjustified, but he never seems to learn from experience, so we hope that the condition is only temporary, and that, when he returns to his abode with the great majority at the end of the séance, his outlook on life there is tinged with a less sombre hue.

However, his pessimism keeps us amused, just as we can be amused by those on earth who are always looking on the black side of things. We try to cheer him up and ask him what he has been doing since we last met, and the conversation proceeds in an animated way, he replying in his quaint English to our remarks. This proceeds for perhaps ten minutes or a quarter of an hour, during which time, so our pessimistic friend tells us, the people in his world are working to set up the means of communication by the Direct Voice. We wait patiently for the result, and are generally not kept too long in suspense.

The talking is proceeding when suddenly a strong voice from somewhere up in the ceiling speaks to us, wishing us "Good evening", to which we reply. Of this new personality we then enquire if we can expect good results, and receive the cheery response that conditions are good and it is hoped that those on his side waiting to speak will manage to get through. Then another voice speaks, telling someone perhaps not to sit with his legs crossed, or reference is made to something which is of interest to someone present. "Mr. Lang, I saw you and Mrs. Lang talking to your gardener yesterday." "Oh, really," replies Mr.

Lang. "Yes, you were telling him that you wanted a rose tree taken from beside the house and put in another part of the garden." "Well, my friend, you are right, I did so; is there anything else you saw or heard?" The conversation continues in an animated way between the voice and Mr. Lang, and ends up by Mr. Lang saying "Well, my friend, though I did not see you, you must have been there as everything you tell me occurred." Then things become more personal, a voice will speak in front of a person present, claiming acquaintanceship, giving both name and earth address, and referring to some personal matter.

I well remember an incident which was very impressive. A voice spoke to a man sitting near me, giving a woman's name, to which he replied. She then referred to his children by name and their various temperaments, and gave some special advice as to how he should deal with the eldest boy who was especially troublesome. Afterwards he told me the voice was that of his recently deceased wife, and she had spoken just as she would have done on earth, knowing all the characteristics of the family, and he concluded with these words: "Neither the medium, nor anyone present, knows anything about me or my family."

Another woman's voice, on this occasion, also spoke to a Colonel McDonald, saying that she was his mother, and had been with him at Communion the previous day at Portree in Skye. He told me afterwards that no one present knew he had just arrived that day from Portree, and that he had attended Communion there the previous day.

Everything is heard by us sitting listening, and so it goes on, one voice after another coming up in front of the person addressed and giving evidence of his or her identity. We may hear, if conditions are good, some thirty or forty different voices speaking to the people present, but, if conditions are bad, only two or three voices speak, and these very indistinctly. Invariably, however, the trumpets are continually moving about the room, when not being spoken through.

I have had them previously rubbed with phosphorus, and thus seen them floating round the room and reaching as high as the ceiling. Sitters are gently touched by them, and, on request, on any part of the body, without mistake, and at the first attempt. No fumbling, always the same clean gentle touch. Then they may give us a musical interlude, either by tapping the trumpets on the floor or by tapping each together. We hear the trumpets go right up to the ceiling and use the ceiling as a drum. Lights of about the size and shape of half-a-crown are moving about the room most of the time, but can never be caught. Always, when you let go your neighbour's hand and try to seize one, it moves away. All this, be it remembered, takes place in complete darkness, and every hand is held round the circle, including the hands of the medium, who never leaves his chair. Normally, it is quite impossible to accomplish.

After a séance I have sat down with others in the dark, and we have attempted to do with the trumpets what we have experienced during the séance, but this point need not be laboured as no one can see in the darkness, and what the trumpets have done during the séance cannot be done by any human being with-out the power of sight. Similarly, no human being in the dark, holding a phosphorescent light, can tell when one of the sitters is going to snatch at it, and withdraw it in time. These phosphorescent lights, like the trumpets, are moved by intelligences to whom our darkness is non-existent, and who belong to a different order of light from that which we experience.

After about three hours it becomes evident that the time is coming when farewells will have to be taken. The voices become less distinct and White-feather tells us that "Not much further more can be said," Whitefeather himself being the last to say "Good-bye." Gradually Sloan comes out of the trance condition, the lights are re-lit, and he invari-ably asks if we have had good results. Throughout it all he has been quite unconscious to everything that has taken place, so the question is a natural one. Very quickly he returns to normal, and we then discuss between ourselves what has taken place.

Such is a description of an average sitting with this remarkable medium. The next morning's news-papers will have nothing to say of what occurred at Sloan's house, though it was of vital interest and importance to every member of the human race. Wireless programmes of the following evening will be eagerly read by wireless enthusiasts, who are eager to hear the voice of someone talking about matters relating to this world in which we live, but no account will be found there of those talks we have had with our friends, who have lived on this earth and passed into another world, who are able to tell us how they are living and what their conditions now are.

We are very much creatures of the present. The next world to many who ever think about it is so distant that it is far beyond their mental grasp. How few of us realise its nearness and the possibility, given the required conditions, of receiving therefrom information and instruction which are just as useful and helpful to mankind as anything that comes from a human voice through our radio transmitter.

CHAPTER VI

THE VOICES

' 'I say with all the strength and force at my command that there is continuity of all life; that nothing is ever lost; that communication is possible, and has been had with those in the after-life in many ways. My effort has been to create a condition in which it became possible for spirit-people to clothe with physical substance their organs of respiration, so they could talk to us when in earth-life. It has been my privilege to hear their voices, best of all methods, hundreds of times. Thousands of individuals have spoken, using their own vocal organs, and I have answered. From this source has come great knowledge, facts beyond the learning of men, nor found in any books, and it is my privilege to give them to you."—RANDALL.

In the last chapter I gave a description of a séance from our point of view, and in this one I shall try to describe it from the view-point of those who spoke to us. What follows is not the product of my imagination. I am telling as clearly as words permit what has been told me by voices which did not belong to this physical world of ours. Every word could be heard distinctly, and was taken down on paper at the time.

Before, however, proceeding further, let us just again understand a little more about ourselves and our physical world. I have already mentioned that much would be said in this book about vibrations, and the person who cannot think in terms of vibrations can no more understand the universe in general, and the particular subject of this book, than a man can understand finance if he has no knowledge of arithmetic. The entire universe is just one gigantic scale of vibrations, but only an infinitesimal number affect our senses.

Let me make this clearer. When we see an object, what we see is its vibrations. These travel to us from the object by means of ether waves, impinge on that extremely sensitive organ, the eye, are thence conveyed to that other sensitive organ, the brain, and from the brain to the mind. The mind then transforms them into a mental image. Our mind is composed of a plastic substance capable of being moulded by these vibrations into a picture, and, when we see a table, it is really not the table we see but the mental image formed in our mind by the vibrations given off by the electrons in the atoms which make up the table.

This will perhaps be better understood if we again go back to our wireless set. We do not hear the speaker's voice in our receiver. His voice vibrates the atmosphere in the room from which he broadcasts. These vibrations affect a drum-like instrument, which in turn retards or accelerates an electric current. This current sends off waves into the ether, which likewise retard or accelerate the electric current passing through our aerial. This current passes through our receiving set and vibrates the drum of the loud speaker. This vibration sets up vibrations in the atmosphere in the room in which we are sitting, which impinge on our ear-drums. Thence they are conveyed to our brain, and then to our mind which produces mental images from what is heard.

So with our sense of touch; the vibrations an article gives off, after passing through our nerves and brain, vibrate our mind, and we have the sensation of touch. Each different substance throws off a different number of vibrations, and we can, by touch, realise if we are holding a wooden object or a cotton fabric, but our sense of touch is not nearly so acute as our sense of sight. So we sometimes cannot by touch alone comprehend what we are touching.

Now the physical world is made up of a certain range of vibrations which affect our senses, but these are only a very small number of the vibrations which are known to exist. The vibrations which make up the physical world we see, vary from about 34,000 to 64,000 waves to the inch, and that is what is called the visible spectrum of the spectroscope, between the Infra Red and the Ultra Violet.

This now brings me to the point I wish to make clear, firstly, that we sense only waves between two fixed points, and secondly that there are an enormous number of vibrations beyond the Ultra Violet and the Infra Red which exist though unsensed by us. Now I come to what I am told about the means used to speak to us by what we call the Direct Voice, by those who have lowered their vibrations for a time and spoken to me on many subjects dealing with their order of life. How is it possible for their higher vibrations to be reduced sufficiently to vibrate our atmosphere?

Let us consider the growth of a child from the moment of conception to the time of death, and then what follows beyond, and if we do so correctly it all becomes much more simple to understand. Conception is only possible when mind associates itself with etheric and physical substances. Mind is of a different order from matter; it is substance—we have no other name for it—vibrating far beyond the Ultra

Violet. This finer substance unites a male cell with a female cell and then development begins.[1]

In the dark, and this is only possible at first in darkness as light would make this materialisation impossible, this finer substance gathers round it physical matter, or, in other words, matter vibrating between the Infra Red and the Ultra Violet. This finer substance thinks from the very start, it forms the framework for the grosser matter to gather round, until a body in due time is formed. After this body is strong enough to withstand our light vibrations, it leaves the darkness and we have what is called birth.

A soul or a mind (either word will do) has arrived to function in the physical world. The process of development continues, physical matter continues to be gathered round the etheric framework, and, along with physical growth, mental growth goes on. This latter never stops, though, as old age comes on, the mind is unable to function with the same ease. However, no matter when death now comes, individuality is definitely established because to the mind belongs the qualities which make us what we are.

The physical head shields the mind from physical vibrations, and this function is likewise performed by the etheric head when we become etheric beings, as in Etheria the mind must be protected from etheric vibrations. It is the individualised mind which produces the individual, and, in fact, is the individual because to it belong the memory, the

---

[1] Every life germ is a trinity, containing mind, etheric matter and physical matter, the two latter constituting the body. Each physical cell has thus a duplicate etheric cell, so that the etheric body is cell for cell similar to the physical body.

affections, and all that makes up our character and personality.

At death the physical garment is discarded to return to earth whence it came, but the mind and the etheric body pass on to a new environment. No change of location occurs immediately, and the etheric being after death remains for a short time in the same place as where death took place. As, however, the etheric body belongs to a higher range of vibrations it now responds to them, and is unable to respond to physical vibrations now that the physical body is discarded. No longer does it sense its physical body, but only the things of the etheric world.

When on earth, matter vibrating within certain fixed limits impinged on the mind through the physical body, but, in the etheric world, vibrations of a higher range impinge on the etheric body and through it to the mind. The mind is then aware of only these higher vibrations, it appreciates the finer structure of the etheric body, and realises the form the body takes, because the etheric body vibrates just as did the physical body. Everything therefore appears to be just as real and solid as it was on earth, because the mind and the etheric body are now functioning in a new range of vibrations with which they are in tune. What to us on earth seems ethereal, and to which we give the name spirit, is not so to the Etherians who regard us on earth in the same etherial way as we regard them.

The earth body, from the time of conception, attached itself to etheric substance which was fashioned according to what the mind directed. Consequently, when the physical body was put aside at death, the same mind still persisted, its hitherto unseen etheric body taking the place of the physical body. The dead man is still alive and unchanged in appearance, and he takes farewell of his old body. Otherwise the only difference to be noticed is the new environment. *Soul* Mind is indestructible, mind persists though death changes its visible covering and environment, but the etheric body has still the form it had on earth, the mind still thinks the same, and remembers its earth experiences.

Even though the physical body was blind through some defect of the eyes, the etheric eyes were not, and after death the etheric eyes can see, and the blind man is blind no longer. Likewise, if the physical body lacked an arm, or a leg, or had other disabilities, the etheric body was unimpaired, and, though the physical limbs were lost, the etheric remained. Nothing is lost through death that is of any value, only a new environment is reached, which environment, to begin with, is just where death occurred.

Consequently death, which has been a mystery and terror to mankind, resolves itself into something which we can now understand, namely that the change of body enables the mind to respond to another order of vibrations. That, and nothing more. We are neither ushered into the presence of God, nor are we annihilated. All that happens is that we sense a new environment, in a body which has always been there encased in the physical body, but it requires the change called death to make us appreciate it. From that event onwards the etheric body responds to these new vibrations. What it cannot do is to rise to a higher plane of vibration than that to which it is fitted to respond, but it can, by thought, respond to lower vibrations right back to those of the physical world.

So we now come to understand how what occurs at a séance is both reasonable and natural. The people of the other world, men and women like ourselves, have their messengers in touch with earth, who report that a séance is to be held, and the news is carried more quickly than is information on earth. The power of thought on these planes of higher vibrations is beyond our capacity to comprehend. Those who wish to speak come back to earth, or lower their vibrations, by gathering round their vocal organs what is called ectoplasm taken from the medium and the sitters. This I shall now explain in greater detail.

To obtain the Direct Voice we require, in conjunction with those in the etheric world, to make the necessary conditions, or otherwise the phenomena will not take place. They on the other side require our co-operation just as much as we require theirs. We are the passive, and they the active co-operators. We require an individual, the medium, possessed with certain vital forces, or substances, to some extent more than normal. To these we, the sitters, supply our own normal vitality.

That constitutes our part in the proceedings, while the rest is done by those who are working with us beyond the veil. As my investigations progressed, so was I impressed with the complications of the procedure in the etheric world which were necessary to produce the conditions to make communication possible. A group of etheric men who are expert in the handling of organic chemical substances work along with us. Immediately we assemble they get to work to do their part.

The group consists of a director of operations, one or more chemists, one who moves the trumpet in the direction an etheric communicator wishes to speak, and one who gathers the substances from the medium and the sitters by connecting them up with the chemist who draws from them the necessary material. This extends from the medium and the sitters to a central point, and the substance drawn from them is gathered by the chemist into an etheric bowl into which he also adds etheric substances of his own. Another of the group helps etheric newcomers to speak, telling them what to do; others keep away those whose only interest in the proceedings is curiosity, and Whitefeather, to whom I have already referred, considers himself the most important of all, as he is detailed off to give warning when a séance is to take place, so that all the operators may be present and at their posts.

Such is a general description of the *modus operandi* of the direct voice, on the physical and on the etheric sides of life, but, given the necessary conditions, what is the explanation of all that takes place?

First of all, we must accept their statement that the etheric body is in every way a duplicate of the physical body, both as regards all internal and external organs. In etheric life, communication takes place in the same way as in earth life. The vocal organs vibrate their atmosphere, the tongue moves, the lungs draw in and expel the equivalent to our air, everything proceeds as it proceeds here on earth, the only difference being that it is all taking place in matter of a much finer structure and at a much more rapid rate of vibration.

Thus their vocal organs, though they can operate in their etheric world, cannot do so in our grosser world. Their texture is too fine for them to have any effect on our atmosphere. New conditions must be created in which vibrations are slower. To obtain these, absolute darkness, or subdued red light, is necessary, as the rays of white light break up and disintegrate those finer forces and substances with which they work. The best results are obtained when the nights are clear, and the atmosphere is free from moisture. At the best the conditions permitting speech are very finely balanced, and, besides the foregoing, the sitters must be in good health and harmonious amongst themselves.

Now let us imagine that we are sitting in a circle, the medium being with us, that by singing we have vibrated the atmosphere for about a quarter of an hour, when suddenly a voice, clear, distinct and away from the medium, breaks in upon us, and, after giving name and earth address, engages one of us in conversation. What has actually happened? It was this question that was always uppermost in my thoughts after I became accustomed to these strange conditions. Was it the medium impersonating someone, or an accomplice among the sitters? For many reasons I became satisfied that this voice did not proceed from any human being, but that there was a personality behind it, which was not one of this world, present in the room. I therefore set myself to find out what actually was the cause behind this effect, and, by a series of questions and answers, over a period of time, was told the following, which, for the sake of brevity, I shall put in my own words.

The chemist, to whom I have already referred, after mixing the substances he obtains from the medium and sitters with his own ingredients, takes the finished preparation and with it first materialises his hands and then forms a rough mask in the likeness of a mouth, throat and lungs. This, when finished, is placed in the most suitable part of the room, often in the centre of the circle. The etheric person (whom we shall call in future the etherian) wishing to speak then presses into this mask, slow in vibration, and with it clothes or covers his mouth, throat, tongue and lungs. These organs then take on a thicker or heavier condition, the tongue requires more exertion to move, but with a little practice it all becomes possible. The speaker then, for the time being, has taken on the necessary conditions to make himself once more such as we are, so far as his capacity to form words which we can hear is concerned.

He is again to this extent an inhabitant of matter, slower in vibration, so that when he speaks he produces the same effects on our atmosphere as we do when we speak. He and we are in the same room, within a few feet of each other, he standing speaking to us, and we sitting, answering. He hears us and we hear him. This condition lasts only for a short time, not often for more than ten minutes. When dematerialisation begins the material falls away, and, though his mouth may continue to speak, he is not heard. This briefly is what they mean by saying that they take on earth conditions from our surroundings.

All direct voice mediums possess a certain vital

force, or substance, all sitters have it in a lesser degree, and to this is added, by the etheric chemists, other etheric forces or substances, the combination of which is a material sufficiently slow in vibration to vibrate our atmosphere. The only thing we cannot understand is how the speaker clothes himself with it, or absorbs it. What is the exact effect which is produced when he presses into it and becomes covered with it? Some day we shall doubtless find out the explanation, but what I write is in substance all that has been told me.

When I have asked for further details I have been told that I would not understand, and must be content with such information as has, so far, been given to me. So I had to be satisfied, but here I again repeat that often I have put my ear quite close to the medium's mouth and heard nothing beyond his regular breathing, though a voice was speaking to someone at the time, and only my personal friends were present in the Séance Room of the Glasgow Society for Psychical Research.

On one occasion the communicator told me that the medium's larynx was being used, and that his voice was being carried by a psychic tube to the trumpet, which magnified it so that we could hear it. In other words, he was making use of the medium's lungs and larynx and mouth to save the necessity of materialising these organs, but even then I did not hear the medium speaking.

This information was made clearer by replies to further questions. When a voice speaks through the trumpet it is not always independent of the medium, and does not always proceed from a materialised entity in the centre of the circle. The power is not always strong enough to maintain this form of communication throughout the entire sitting. What happens is this. The communicator who wishes to speak controls the medium and speaks through him. The communicator has not, however, the same control over the medium as his regular controllers, and the voice produced is sometimes not above a whisper. The voice is conveyed from the medium's mouth by means of a materialised ectoplasmic or psychic tube to the trumpet, which amplifies the voice so that it can be heard. Speaking under these circumstances the speaker stands behind the medium, whose etheric body for the time being is detached from his physical body; in other words the medium is in trance. The communicator is thus able to control the medium's vocal organs.

There is an etheric connecting link, which has the same effect on the medium's muscles as the atmospheric waves have on two tuning forks tuned to the same pitch. As the vibrations of one act on the other, so the two sets of vocal organs, those of the etheric speaker and those of the medium, act in unison. Thus what the etherian says the medium says, both sets of organs working in harmony.

That information satisfied me up to a point, but the question was how the sound was produced. Our lips form the words, our larynx causes the sound. I then asked what caused the sound, and was told that the medium's larynx was used for this purpose, and that the sound was conveyed from it by means of the etheric tube to the trumpet. It was made clear, however, that what was carried from the medium to the trumpet was not air from the medium's lungs. The larynx is used to cause the sound, but not by means of air passing through the vocal chords. The atmosphere is vibrated by a method of their own, and I was told I must accept the fact that the larynx was used to produce the sound, which was carried to the trumpet from the etherian who was speaking.

There is no question, my informant insisted, of the messages in any way being influenced by the medium's mind, as his mind does not come into the question at all. They do not act through the medium's mind, but directly on his vocal organs. The mind of the etheric speaker is in complete control, and the medium's brain is switched off for the time being. What we sometimes hear, therefore, is the medium's voice through the trumpet, though it sounds quite unlike his own, as it always does in trance, and this form of communication is different from the Direct Voice, because the voice is conveyed to the trumpet and not produced quite apart from the medium. At times they tell me that they can convey the voice into the trumpet right across the circle.

At Sloan's séances we have, therefore, three different forms of communication. Firstly, trance utterances. Secondly, by means of the method just described; and thirdly, the best of all, voices from etheric men, women and children who have material-ised their vocal organs and lungs and speak as we do, without any connection whatever with the medium, except the ectoplasmic substance necessary for materi-alisation which they borrow from the medium and sitters.

The trumpet is moved by materialised rods, made

by a combination of these substances supplied by the medium, the sitters, and their chemist. It can be moved also by a materialised hand, and the larger end is used to rest the materialised mouth on, inside the trumpet, thus directing the voice in the direction the speaker desires to speak without his requiring to move from the place where he has materialised. Either end of the trumpet can be used, whichever suits their purpose best. When the trumpet is not used it means that the substance is sufficient, and the power strong enough, to enable one or more materialisations to take place, usually in the vicinity of the person to whom the communicator wishes to speak. Thus, I have heard, on occasion, two and sometimes three voices speaking to different people at the same time.

Not always, however, is the person present who purports to speak, as those who have passed through what is called the second transition, on to a higher plane of thought, find it difficult, if not impossible, to communicate. They, however, can communicate with those in the lower plane, their messages being picked up and passed on by some Etherian present at the séance. This, I think, is often done, even by those on the surface of the sphere bordering this earth who find communication difficult by means of materialising their own vocal organs. An Irishman in etheric life, named Gallacher, told me that much of his time at a séance was occupied in taking messages and passing them on. He calls himself the "telephone exchange".

I asked once if the materialised vocal organs could be touched and had weight, and was told they could be, and that they had the weight that we, the sitters,

had lost during the sitting. If we each sat on a weigh-
ing machine we would find our weight during the
séance gradually decreasing, and, as the séance neared
an end, as the ectoplasm was returned, so would our
weight return to normal. The experiments by Dr.
Crawford, and others, have proved this statement to
be correct. This ectoplasm, which they draw from us,
is useless unless it is mixed with ingredients supplied
by the chemist, as materialisation could not take place
from ectoplasm alone.

This ectoplasmic-etheric combination is, I am told,
the preparation required, not only for materialisation,
but for the movement by those in the other world of all
physical objects. They can move nothing on earth without it. Our bodies are composed of the ingredients
from which they draw this substance called ectoplasm.
I have found it impossible, however, to get any detailed
information as to what are the chemical ingredients
of the substance they add to the ectoplasm. The
chemist would not tell me, as he said I could not understand even if he did. I asked once if the thoughts
of the medium in any way coloured the communications which came by means of the direct voice, and
the reply I received was, "Certainly not".

As to what takes place when the medium speaks
in trance, I am told that the etherian wishing to speak
gathers ectoplasm from the medium, and thus gets
control of his vocal organs. So far as Sloan is concerned, his brain is not used in any way. What happens
is briefly this. The ectoplasm forms the connecting
link between the etherian speaking and the medium's
vocal organs, and, as the etherian speaks, so the
medium's vocal organs move. Here materialisation

of the mouth, throat and tongue does not take place, the medium's vocal organs being used to vibrate the atmosphere, and form the words spoken by the controlling etheric man, woman or child.

My claim for this book is that it gives an explanation, both logical and reasonable, of how the phenomenon of the Direct Voice occurs, and one which should appeal to everyone. Evidence, such as is contained in the next four chapters, may not in itself be sufficient to convince the average individual, but, when a logical explanation can also be given, an acceptance of the phenomenon is much less difficult. I have created conditions so as to make fraud and impersonation impossible, and, by persistent enquiry, have obtained information about the Etheric World, its inhabitants, and how communication takes place which should satisfy the average individual.

This has never been attempted before, to my knowledge, in the same systematic way, but it must be remembered that I have dealt with hard facts all my life. I have required a knowledge of economics and mathematics in my business life, and, outside of this, my special interest has been in physics. I have therefore approached this subject in a matter-of-fact way, and have obtained information which makes the phenomena, to any unbiased person, both reasonable and natural. Consequently this enquiry should help to raise the study of psychic phenomena to a higher plane of thought, and be another stepping stone towards its being ultimately placed on a strictly scientific basis.

CHAPTER VII

MY FIRST EVIDENCE

"The search for truth is the noblest occupation of man, and its publication
is a duty".—DE STAËL.

THE previous chapters must be considered in the light
of an introduction to the subject of this book. I now
come to the kernel of the whole affair, namely, the
evidence, and it is on the evidence that everything
rests and the whole argument is built up.

It may be contended that the evidence should have
come first and the deductions last, but, in a case such
as this, one has to prepare the ground so that the
possibility of communication is primarily accepted,
and what takes place at a séance understood.

In 1918 my wife became seriously ill and had to be
removed to a nursing home in Glasgow, where she
had an operation, from which she recovered and was
fortunately none the worse. To be near to her I
stayed in Glasgow, and, when sitting with her one
Sunday evening, I remarked that I would like some
fresh air and would go out for a stroll. Little did I
think what that walk would mean to me, but it was the
beginning of an entire change in my mental outlook
on life and death.

I sauntered down one street and up another rather
aimlessly, to pass a church with the name "Spiritualist
Church" prominently displayed in the foreground. I
stopped to see what it looked like, as I did not remember having seen it before, and I was unaware that
such a denomination existed. What little I knew of

Spiritualism was contained in a book my wife had recently been given and which to me, by a casual glance, seemed too fantastic for serious thought. I threw it aside as not worth reading, and now that Sunday evening I was facing the entrance to a Spiritualist church. Why not enter and see what it is like inside? I thought, and this I did.

A service was going on and the speaker was telling the congregation of some wonderful things he had experienced. I sat down and listened, and when the service was over I went up to him and this is what I said: "Do you really expect me to believe what you said tonight? It may have gone down with some simple-minded people who listened to you, but do you expect a rational thinker to accept as true what you said? Can you prove it to me?"

I have from time to time challenged a parson with questions, and have received as a reply: "No, I can prove nothing, but that is where faith comes in. You must believe and not doubt." The Spiritualist, whom I now challenged, said exactly the opposite, to the effect that I could not be expected to believe without proof. "Proof is essential," he continued, "and what Spiritualists believe has come from experience. All claims made by Spiritualists can be proved, and if you want to have proof you can get it." "How?" I enquired. "By going to a medium," he answered. "Can you take me to one?" I asked. "Yes, tomorrow night, if that is convenient to you," he replied.

That reply appealed to me, and I accepted his offer. So it was arranged that the following night I would meet him at seven o'clock at the corner of

North Frederick Street and George Street, and he would take me to a séance which was held every Monday evening in a house nearby. When I returned and told my wife where I was about to go, she wondered if it were a wise thing to do. To go with a strange man to a strange house seemed to her taking an unjustifiable risk, but she raised no objection and I kept the appointment next day as arranged.

Consequently on the following day, Monday, 20th September 1918, we met at the place arranged and walked along a quiet street to a house, the entrance to which was by a passage. He told me we were going to the house of John Sloan, who was a medium. We entered the passage, and my unknown guide knocked at the door on the right-hand side. It was opened, and we were ushered into a small room in which were ten people, all sitting on chairs in a circle. The light was on and talking was general. A man was playing a hymn on a harmonium. We were both given seats in the circle and no introductions were made. All that was said by my guide was a remark to the man at the harmonium that he had brought someone with him. That was all. My guide did not know my name, I did not know his, and the rest of the people were all complete strangers to me. I put them down as belonging to what is called the working class, nice, kindly, decent people who gave me a very friendly welcome.

The man at the harmonium then said it was time to start, and he switched off the light. A hymn was played and sung and then another, but before it ended the organist turned round and took his place in the circle. Shortly after this a man's loud voice spoke right in front of my right-hand neighbour. I heard everything said and the name it gave, the conversation being an intimate one between my female neighbour and this voice. She had evidently spoken to the voice before, and took it all quietly and naturally. The voice seemed to know everything of importance she had done since the last conversation, and ended with love and the promise to be back again at the next séance.

When the voice had finished speaking, she calmly announced to everyone that she had been speaking to her husband, whom I took to be dead. This went on for three hours, dozens of voices speaking to different people, men's voices, women's voices, children's voices, all of which I was told came from people called dead. A woman's voice spoke to a man sitting on my left. It gave a name and referred to happenings at his home. It specially referred to Tom, who was giving his father trouble, and then came advice as to how he should be dealt with. Intimate family matters were discussed between my neighbour and this female voice, and finally with love it said "Goodbye". "That was my wife," he whispered to me. "I never come here but she comes back to me. She always knows everything that goes on at home."

I was now beginning to feel that I was the only one to be omitted from this strange medley of conversation which seemed to go on and on without stopping. Everything said was claimed to be correct, and I wondered how it was possible for any human being to be so intimate with all the dead friends, and the private doings of the sitters, as to be able to impersonate their deceased relations in the way that was taking place.

Not only did the imagined impersonator know intimately about their dead friends and relations but every voice was different, the mannerisms were different, in fact each voice had a different personality. What a wonderful actor there must be amongst us to be able to carry on like this for hours on end, and to remember in the dark where everyone was sitting, as the right person was directly addressed every time with never a mistake.

Such were my thoughts, when suddenly right in front of my face a strong voice spoke to me. "Yes, who are you?" I enquired, to receive the answer:

"Your father, Robert Downie Findlay."

The voice continued speaking, and referred to something that only my father and I, and one other man, ever knew about on earth, and that other man, like my father, was dead. I was therefore the only living person on earth with any knowledge of what the voice was talking about. It was a private matter that neither I, nor my father, nor any other man when on earth, ever spoke about to any other person. All this was extraordinary enough, but imagine my surprise when my father concluded by saying:

"David Kidston is standing beside me and would also like to talk to you about this matter."

Now David Kidston was the name of the other man who knew about this private affair. He was my father's partner, and he was my partner after my father's death. Only the three of us knew about this private affair and here I was in a Glasgow artisan's house, a complete stranger to everyone, being told by two different voices about something known only to me and two dead men. Moreover, the voices

which spoke claimed to be the voices of these two men,
and Kidston continued the conversation quite naturally which my father had started, to conclude with
these words:

"I am glad to get that off my chest at last."

When I first wrote *On the Edge of the Etheric* I included in it this experience and others I had with this
medium, but I gave no details as to what the voices
said to me on this occasion. I thought it wiser then
to give an outline of what happened and no more, as
to recount what the voice, which claimed to come
from my father, said and what the voice, claiming to
come from Kidston, said, would have involved too
much explanation before the matter could be understood. However, now that my past life has been
made public in my autobiography *Looking Back* there
is no reason why everything should not be told.

What my father said after giving his name was this:

"I am very sorry I did not take you into my business. I would have liked to do so but Kidston opposed
it. If you had been with me it would have greatly
eased my life, as I found business a great strain on me.
David Kidston is standing beside me and would also
like to talk to you about this matter."

Then a voice claiming to be that of David Kidston
spoke, saying:

"I am David Kidston. I was wrong opposing your
coming into our office. I am sorry I did it but now you
need have no regrets. I am glad to get that off my
chest at last."

That was all true, but only my father, myself, and
Kidston knew about it, and the incident referred to
happened when my grandfather died in 1904, fourteen

years previously. When he passed on, I said to my father that I would like to enter Findlay, Kidston & Goff's office, as now my prospects of becoming a partner in Patrick Henderson & Co. were not so bright. My grandfather's influence had gone, and I might have to wait years before I became a partner. My father agreed, and said he would speak to Kidston about it as I would be a great help to him. My disappointment was great when he told me that Kidston would not agree, because the business earned enough for only three partners. He evidently foresaw the day when my father would want me to become a partner, and that would mean less to go round.

Kidston was so short-sighted that he could not foresee me bringing in enough new business to the firm to justify my being made a partner, but he was a very difficult man to work with and my father had some unpleasant times with him. He was gruff, short in his manner and domineering, so much so that my father rather feared him. So I knew that what Kidston had said was final and I never raised the matter again, but, as neither he nor Goff had sons, I saw something good slipping away from me. So my request and its refusal remained known only to us three. Nevertheless, here was I listening to what had happened fourteen years previously, in a strange house, and in the company of people I had never seen before in my life.

That indeed was a problem. No spy system, however thorough it was, no fraud or impersonation by the medium or anyone else could be responsible for what I had experienced. I was up against something quite inexplicable. That, then, was my first introduction to Spiritualism, and, when the séance was over, I was introduced to the medium, John Campbell Sloan, the man who was at the harmonium when I entered. I thanked him for his hospitality, and asked him if I could come back again, as I was anxious to know more about this subject.

I left Sloan's house in company with the man who took me there, and he accepted my experience as a matter of course. "That is how people become Spiritualists," he said. "I told you I could prove to you what I said last night, and, you see, I have done so." He told me his name was Duncan McPherson, and I found out later that he was a much respected leader in the Glasgow Spiritualist movement, he himself being a medium. Some years later he died and returned to a séance at which my brother was present in Manchester. He, McPherson, spoke to my brother and said that it was he who had taken me to my first séance after meeting me at the Scottish Mediums' Union Church one Sunday evening. My brother replied: "I think you are wrong, you met my brother at the Holland Street Spiritualist Church."

"No, I did not," was the reply, "it was at the Scottish Mediums' Union Church, 100, West Regent Street, I first met your brother and I took him the next day to Sloan's. Ask your brother and you will find out that I am right."

So my brother asked me next time we met. He was wrong, and the voice claiming to be that of McPherson was right. It was at the Scottish Mediums' Union Church that we first met, so that telepathy, if telepathy can produce a voice, which it can't do, is not the explanation of how this happened.

During the next five years I attended thirty-nine séances with Sloan, sometimes at his house and at times in places of my own choosing. Eighty-three separate voices have spoken to me or to friends I have taken with me. I have given details in this book of the precautions I took to make sure it was not Sloan who was speaking. I sat with him at times alone and the voices spoke even when my ear was within an inch of his mouth, which was silent. Two and three voices sometimes spoke at the same time. Occasionally the voices were so strong that they could be heard across the street. The most convincing experiences were when I took strangers to a séance. Sloan knew nothing about them and I never mentioned their names. Here are a few instances which come under this category.

One evening I took with me the widow of a man whose body had been cremated that day and whose funeral I attended. I introduced her to Sloan by another name. A voice spoke to me when the séance began:

"Why did you give the lady's wrong name? We know who she is, and her husband, Louis Pearson, is here to speak to her."

Pearson then spoke, remarking that it would take him some time to recover from seeing his earth body burned. When speaking to his wife he became very emotional, so much so that he could not continue his conversation with her, much to her disappointment.

On another occasion I took with me a professor from Glasgow University. I did not give his name, I knew little about him, but his experience interested me. A voice spoke to him in a language I did not understand. He replied in the same language, and the conversation went on for some time. After the séance was over I asked him what language he was speaking. He replied: "I was speaking Welsh, I am Welsh, and the voice which spoke to me gave the name of an old gardener I employed when I lived in Wales. He knew all about me and what he said was quite true."

These two experiences I have never recorded before, nor the fact that my father came back on other occasions and gave me good evidence of his presence and survival, but I could go on and on. Some of my experiences can be found related in my books, others I have never publicly told, in fact I have dozens of similar incidents hidden away in my memory or on record, which are as evidential as any I have published.

Many departed friends and relations have returned and given their correct names, and good evidence of their survival, but nothing was more amazing than the return of Eric Saunders, as will be reported. Not only was his evidence remarkable, and everything checked later as correct, but he was seen when speaking.

The Hon. Everard Fielding, who was such an active member of the Society for Psychical Research, once wrote to me to say that a friend of his would be coming to Glasgow, and would very much like to have a sitting with Sloan. I replied that I would arrange this, and, on the day appointed, Mr. Fielding's friend called to see me at my office. In the evening he dined with me at my club, after which we went to Sloan's house where the sitting was held. This man, during the course of our conversation prior to the séance, never gave me a hint of his occupation, and I purposely asked him no particulars. He was therefore a complete stranger to me, and neither I, nor the medium, nor anybody present at the séance, knew anything about him.

The séance was a good one, and during it a voice spoke clearly and distinctly before my new acquaintance. It addressed him correctly, and, when he asked who was speaking, the voice replied:

"When on earth I was known as King Edward VII."

A personal conversation ensued, names of people being mentioned by the voice which my acquaintance knew, and the conversation went on quite naturally just as if my friend were speaking to someone on earth. Finally, the voice said:

"I must thank you for all your kindness to my wife, Queen Alexandra. I do not know how she could have gone on without you, and you have relieved her of much worry and care."

After the séance was over I asked him if he were satisfied with his strange experience, and he replied: "Most certainly." Then I said, "Will you tell me what your position is towards Queen Alexandra?" "Oh," he replied, "I am the Controller of her household." Neither I, nor any other person in the room that night except himself knew this, and it therefore follows that the voice that spoke to him was not of this world. Moreover, the person who controlled the voice knew all about him and his friends, which proves that someone, unseen to us, was present with knowledge beyond that of the medium, myself, and the other regular sitters.

Queen Alexandra, when she heard about this séance, wanted to sit with Sloan and this took place in London. I am glad to say that this gave her great satisfaction. Those also present were my friends, Sir William Barrett the eminent physicist, Sir Arthur Conan Doyle, Dr. Abraham Wallace and Sir Oliver Lodge, all believers in the reality of this phenomena after years of study and experience. Besides them were Sir Thomas Lipton and Marconi, for whose opinions I cannot vouch. Lastly, there was Mr. Byrd, the American scientist who did not believe in survival, but he came, he said, with an open mind. A friend of his came back, giving his name, and spoke to him, reminding him of the occasion when they were both together on Brooklyn Bridge and what they then talked about. The voice repeated parts of the conversation they had on the bridge and to this Byrd replied "That is all true, but how can you speak to me when you are dead?"

When we came south to live at Stansted Hall, a friend and near neighbour of ours was the late Frances, Countess of Warwick, a charming woman and overflowing with human kindness. I told her about King Edward coming back to speak to the Controller of Queen Alexandra's household and she replied: "King Edward has often come back to speak to me. We were friends, and when he was on earth we always spoke to each other in German. After his death he has come back to me at séances, and always spoke to me by the direct voice. Just as he always spoke German to me on earth, so he spoke to me in German at these séances."

I wish I could give details of one more very evidential conversation which took place. My wife was once with me at a séance with Sloan, when a woman's voice spoke to her and said who she was. I would like to say who she was and what the voice said to my wife about a very personal matter, but I cannot do so as it is much too private. What is important is that only the one claiming to be the person she said she was could have known about it, and what she said to my wife was true and very appropriate. No one present could possibly have known about the matter to which the speaker referred.

I would mention here that Sloan on acquaintance impressed me always as an upright, good, honest man, with little learning, a bad memory and just the average intelligence common to his class. He was a packer at a Glasgow warehouse, and his employer, who was a frequent sitter at his séances, told me he was a trustworthy, upright man. This was the opinion of the very many other people who knew him, and I never once heard uttered a word of suspicion about the honest conduct of his séances.

Over five years I accumulated so much evidence of survival after death that I wrote and published this book eight years later. I gave many public lectures and once spoke on my experiences to the members of the Glasgow Philosophical Society at their headquarters, the meeting being packed, and my chairman was the senior Law Lord of the Court of Session. Then, on the suggestion of a lady, Miss Irwin, I formed the Glasgow Society for Psychical Research, a professor of the University becoming President and I the Vice-President. This new society had regular private meetings of members and arranged public ones, one being in the St. Andrew's Hall, where two thousand people heard the eminent physicist Sir William Barrett. I had the honour of being chairman, and remember Barrett in his speech recalling that forty years earlier in the same hall, at a meeting of the British Association, he had advocated the investigation of telepathy, but that no one gave him any support.

CHAPTER VIII

THE EVIDENCE: THREE "A1" CASES

"Nothing can destroy the evidence of testimony in any case but a proof or probability that persons are not competent judges of the facts to which they give testimony, or that they are actually under some indirect influence in giving it in such particular case. Till this is made out the testimony must be admitted."—Butler.

In this chapter I shall give a summary of three cases that I class as "A1", and, in the next, of three I class as "A2". They are only summaries, as I have only space sufficient to enable me to dwell upon the salient points of each.

Case 1 of the "A 1" Group.—I took my brother with me to a séance shortly after he was demobilised from the Army in 1919. He knew no one present, and was not introduced. No one present, except myself, knew that he had been in the Army. No one present knew where he had been during his time in the Army. His health had not permitted him to go abroad, and he was stationed part of the time near Lowestoft at a small village called Kessingland, and part of the time at Lowestoft, training gunners. With this preliminary explanation I shall now give you the following summary of my notes on this case:

During the course of the sitting the trumpet was distinctly heard moving about the room, and various voices spoke through it. Suddenly it tapped my brother on the right knee, and a voice directly in front of him said, "Eric Saunders". My brother asked if the voice were addressing him, and it replied "Yes", whereupon he said that there must be some mistake, as he had never known anybody of that name. The voice was not very strong, so some person suggested that the company should continue singing, and, while this was going on, the trumpet kept tapping my brother on his knee, arm and shoulder. It was so insistent that he said : "I think we had better stop singing, as some person evidently is most anxious to speak to me."

Again he asked who it was, and the voice, much stronger this time, repeated, "Eric Saunders". Again my brother said that he had never known any person of that name, and asked where he had met him. The reply was: "In the Army." My brother mentioned a number of places, such as Aldershot, Bisley, France, Palestine, etc., but carefully omitted Lowestoft, where he had been stationed for the greater part of his army life. The voice replied "No, none of these places. I knew you when you were *near* Lowestoft." My brother asked why he said "*Near* Lowestoft," and he replied: "You were not in Lowestoft then, but at Kessingland."

This is a small fishing hamlet about five miles south of Lowestoft, where my brother spent part of 1917. My brother then asked what company he had been attached to, and, as he could not make out whether he said "B" or "C", my brother asked if he could remember the name of the Company Commander. The reply was "Macnamara". This was the name of the officer commanding "B" Company at that time.

By way of a test, my brother pretended that he remembered the man, and said: "Oh yes, you were one of my Lewis gunners, were you not?" The reply was: "No, you had not the Lewis guns then, it was the Hotchkiss." This was quite correct, as the Lewis guns were taken from them in April 1917, and were replaced by Hotchkiss. My brother asked him two or three leading questions, such as the name of his (my brother's) billet, which he answered correctly, and then Saunders said: "We had great times there, sir; do you remember the General's inspection?" My brother laughed, and said that they were continually being inspected by generals, to which one did he refer, and he replied: "The day the General made us all race about with the guns."

This was an incident my brother remembered perfectly well, and one which caused a good deal of amusement to the men at the time. He told my brother he had been killed in France, and my brother asked him when he had gone out. He replied that he had gone with the "Big Draft in August 1917". My brother asked him why he called it the Big Draft, and he said: "Don't you remember the Big Draft, when the Colonel came on the parade ground and made a speech." This reference was to a particularly large draft sent out to France that month, and was the only occasion on which my brother remembered the Colonel ever personally saying good-bye to the men.

He then thanked my brother for the gunnery training he had given him, and said it had been most useful to him in France. My brother asked him why he had come through to speak to him, and he said: "Because I have never forgotten that you once did me a good turn." My brother has a hazy recollection of obtaining leave for one of the gunners, owing to some special circumstances, but whether or not his name was "Saunders" he could not remember.

About six months after the above incident my brother was in London, and met, by appointment, the Corporal who had been his assistant with the light guns in his battalion at that time. My brother told him the above story, and asked if he remembered any man named "Eric Saunders". My brother had been training gunners for nearly two years at the rate of about a dozen a fortnight, and, beyond putting them through their examinations, and taking a general oversight of them, he never came into sufficiently close personal contact with them to get to know many of their names. The Corporal, however, whom my brother met, was more with the gunners, but he did not remember any person of this name.

Fortunately, however, the Corporal had brought with him an old pocket diary, in which he had been in the habit of keeping a full list of men under training, and other information. He pulled it out of his pocket, and together they looked back until they came to the records of "B" Company during 1917. Sure enough the name appeared there, "Eric Saunders, f.q., August '17", with a red-ink line drawn through it; f.q. stood for fully qualified, and, though my brother knew the meaning of the red-ink line, he asked the Corporal what it meant. He replied: "Don't you remember, Mr. Findlay, I always drew a line through the men's names when they went away. This shows that Saunders went out in August 1917."

Unfortunately my brother did not ask Saunders the name of his regiment, and consequently I could not trace his death, the War Office, without this information, being unable to supply me with any details beyond the fact that over 4,000 men of the name of Saunders fell in the War. Men came to Lowestoft from all over the country for training, so my brother had no record of Saunders' regiment.

Even allowing for this it is a remarkable case, as it is fraud proof, telepathy proof, and cryptæsthesia proof. Not only did no one present know my brother, but my brother did not know the speaker, and cannot even to-day recollect him, as he was passing hundreds of men through their training, all of whom would know him, but he never had an opportunity to know them individually. This case contains fourteen separate facts; each one was correct, and each one comes up to my "A1" standard. Clairvoyants present described Saunders standing in front of us speaking, and, with a smile, saluting my brother before he left us.

I shall now give another "A1" case:

CASE 2 "A1".—One day when in Edinburgh I visited the Rev. John Lamond, D.D., a friend of mine, and noticed an oil painting on his study mantelpiece. Remarking on it, I was told that it was a painting by the trance painter, David Duguid, who died in the early part of this century. "It has a history," my friend told me, and then went on to say: "I had that painted once, many years ago when I visited David Duguid in Glasgow, and, as my family did not believe in this method of painting, I promptly put it in a tin box." Some years later, after the death of Duguid, my friend was at a direct voice séance in London, and a voice spoke to him giving the name David Duguid. "You surely do not value my painting, Dr. Lamond," said

David. "Why?" said my friend. "If you did, you would not keep it in a box in your room." My friend had forgotten where he had put it, but told Duguid that he would search for it and put it on his mantelpiece. Just as Duguid had said, it was in the box referred to, and my friend kept his promise and placed it on his mantelpiece.

This was the story I was told the day I visited Dr. Lamond in Edinburgh. I never mentioned it to anyone, and he did not know Sloan. Now for the sequel. Some time after the story of the picture was told to me I took to one of Sloan's séances Dr. W. P. Paterson, Professor of Divinity at Edinburgh University and former Moderator of the General Assembly of the Church of Scotland. He had never heard the story from his friend Dr. Lamond, who is rather sensitive about touching on a subject in which his friends disbelieve. However, Dr. Paterson came with me to Sloan's house one night. He sat beside me, and was not introduced to anyone present. He had never seen Sloan before, and Sloan certainly did not know him.

First of all he received some remarkable evidence, and then a strong voice boomed out and addressed him by name. "Dr. Paterson," it said, "I am David Duguid; tell your friend Dr. Lamond, 18 Regent Terrace, Edinburgh (correct), that I am much obliged to him for keeping his promise and placing my picture on his mantelpiece." Dr. Paterson was quite bewildered, and, addressing me, said: "I don't know what he is talking about." I, however, knowing the story, promised Duguid to deliver the message, for which I received his thanks. This is another fool-proof case and can be rightly classed "A1", it being quite free from any other explanation than that the personality of Duguid was present, and spoke. Otherwise how could such a message have come?

CASE 3 "A1".—The last "A1" case I shall give relates to a lady, Mrs. Wood Sims, whom I took with me one evening. Sloan's séance was timed to begin at 7.15, and on my way to it I called on the lady and asked her if she would care to come with me. As it was then past seven she hurriedly got ready and came with me. She mentioned casually to me that she had just returned from a visit to friends in England, and I heard her make the same remark to someone just before the séance began, but no details were given—just the casual remark.

During the séance a voice spoke to her, giving the name of her host's deceased son, saying: "I saw you when you were staying with father at Leeds." Several other voices spoke to her, giving their names, and sent messages to her host at Leeds. Two of these she did not know, but she said she would tell her host they had spoken, and pass on their messages.

Mrs. Wood Sims afterwards told me that her host had replied that he had known all these people on earth, and their messages were quite intelligible to him. [At a later date I met this gentleman, and he confirmed what Mrs. Wood Sims told me.] This lady's brother, also on this occasion, spoke to her, calling her "Anna", a name only he used, as she is never called by that name. He said his name was "Will", but "Bill" to her, which was correct, and then correctly referred in detail to some advice he gave her before his death. "If you had only taken it, how different your life would have been," he said. "It is only too true," said my friend to me afterwards. Finally, his face materialised before her, and she assures me that it was his face in every detail.

Here we have fourteen "A1" facts recorded, and these three cases I have mentioned, containing thirty-four "A1" facts, are only three of many. Remember, in my notes, I have on record one hundred and eighty facts, every one as good as those to which I have referred.

Taking, however, these three cases, fraud is excluded, owing to the precautions taken. What of chance, in other words, guessing on the part of the medium? An eminent mathematician, on calculating the chances of correctly guessing all the facts recorded, considers that to have reached such accuracy represented the equivalent of 1 to 5,000,000,000,000; in other words, the odds were 5,000,000,000,000 to 1 against chance being the explanation. That being so we need scarcely consider it.

CHAPTER IX

MORE EVIDENCE: THREE "A2" CASES

"Truth comes to us with a slow and doubtful step; measuring the ground
she treads on, and for ever turning her curious eye to see that all is
right behind; and with a keen survey choosing her onward path."—
PERCIVAL.

I SHALL now summarise three cases which I class
"A2", as they do not come under quite the same
category as my "A1" cases, though it by no means
follows that the information was normally obtained.
All I mean is that some of the information was available normally, and, this being so, critics are open to
give this as an explanation.

CASE 1 "A2".—I arranged a sitting with Sloan
one evening in our Society's rooms in Glasgow,
and mentioned to him the name of a friend of mine
who was coming. As things turned out I was sorry
I did so, as, if I had not, it would have been a wonderful "A1" sitting. He was a London man, and his
wife came with him. He was well known as a Spiritualist and a leader in finance. His name, career and
certain family matters were mentioned in *Who's Who*.
This cannot explain all that took place, but just because his name was known I cannot class the case as
"A1". However, at least seven different voices spoke
to him and his wife. They referred to family matters,
gave family names and showed an intimate knowledge
of his public and home life. He told me afterwards
that, though he had studied the phenomena for twenty
years, it was one of the most evidential and interesting
sittings in which he had ever taken part.

CASE. 2 "A2".—A lady, a friend of mine, died. She belonged to a well-known family. Consequently an obituary notice of about a quarter of a column appeared in the *Glasgow Herald*, giving particulars of her family and immediate ancestors. This, consequently, brings this case under the "A2" category, though I know of nothing to associate her with me or my family in the mind of the medium. Sloan, I am sure, was not aware that I knew her. I am sure Sloan had never heard her name and knew nothing about her or her family, but, as some critics make out that a case loses its evidentiality if the information given can be traced to print, I place this one accordingly in the "A2" category.

A week after her funeral, at a sitting I and a few personal friends had with Sloan in the séance room of our Society, her son, Cecil, who was killed in the war, spoke to my brother saying that he was so happy now, as he had his mother with him. I asked if she were present, and he replied she was, but not yet fully conscious that she had passed over. I asked if she could speak to me, which she did.

Her conversation showed that she was not quite conscious of the change. She said she wanted her husband, naming him correctly, referred to the nature of her illness correctly, and wanted to know what had happened. I might add that the nature of her illness had not been published, and was only known to a few of her intimate friends. I explained to her the change which had taken place, that she was now an inhabitant of the etheric world, that she had left for ever this world of physical matter, that she had gone through the change called death, and then I said, "Do you not recognise who is standing beside you?" referring to her son who had just spoken to me. "No," she said, "I can see no one." Here her son interposed with the remark. "Mother cannot recognise me yet."

Her father then spoke to me, telling me things I afterwards found in reference books to be correct. Then her brother spoke, giving his correct name and where he lived on earth. Towards the end of the séance, after other voices had spoken, the lady returned and again spoke to me. "Have you not seen Cecil?" I said. "No; where is he?" she replied. Then her voice suddenly changed from one of sadness to joy, and we heard her exclaim, "Oh, Cecil, my darling my own darling boy." Then there was silence. In a few minutes another voice spoke: "He is taking her away with him; she will soon be all right."

I had been a participant in a great drama. I had been privileged to have the unique experience of witnessing the return to consciousness of one the world called "dead", and her meeting with her son, who had given, so the world thought, his life for his country. I had witnessed, when she was with us on earth, her terrible grief when she had heard of his death, her wonderful courage, and I was present at the final act when she and her only son became reunited. How I should have liked to tell her sorrowing husband of my experience, but I knew how useless it was, so I refrained from doing so.

To describe, in a few words, what took nearly two hours to unfold, to make one conscious of the rare personal touches which accompanied it all, is, of course, impossible. The circle consisted entirely of my own personal friends, in the séance room of our own

Society, and they were all deeply affected, especially my wife who knew the lady well. Had Sloan been a great actor, knowing intimately the personalities concerned, and their family history, he could not have carried through, with such success, the various impersonations, whereas he knew nothing about her or her family, or my friendship with her and her son.

CASE 3 "A2".—This is a peculiar case. I class it "A2" as it is unevidential, but I mention it because I cannot believe its source was other than super-normal. I may say, by way of explanation, that a scientific group, on the other side, has taken a great interest in my investigations, and given me all the help they could. Later I shall have something of interest to say with regard to the scientific views they expressed from time to time. Huxley, Faraday, Alfred Russel Wallace, and other scientists, first of all started to come through to me after I took Sloan in London to see Sir William and Lady Barrett who had known some of them personally. Immediately after that, Lady Barrett was present at two sittings with Sloan in London, one following the other, when Huxley and other scientists first began to manifest, sending their best wishes and congratulations to their old friend, her husband, for his persistency in keeping the fact of survival before the public. Huxley and others evidently kept in touch with me, as from that time onwards they repeatedly spoke to me. Huxley especially has given me good proof of his identity in a most evidential manner. His personal appearance has also been accurately described.

I mention these facts by way of explaining why I have had so much attention from this group, but one will realise that I must qualify my statement by saying that I have only their word for it that they are the men who bore these great names on earth. With those who speak, whom you never knew, you lose the personal touches which are so convincing when they come from friends. Now I shall tell my story.

On 10th December 1923, I received a note from Sloan saying: "Before penning these lines I have the influence of a quiet man beside me who says, 'Write to Mr. Findlay to have no fear: we shall see that he acquits himself well at the forthcoming meeting, and we will have him well informed in all matters before the meeting.' I get something like *Raleigh* as his name." This was Sloan's letter to me, the meeting referred to was one I was addressing in the lecture hall of the Glasgow Philosophical Society, and it should be noted how he spells the name.

I sat with Sloan the following evening, and, in the dark, before he went into trance, he described a man standing beside me. Then he said he saw letters flashed above my head which he could make nothing of. I asked him to read them out one by one, while I noted them down. This he did very quickly, spelling them out as follows: *hgielyarmai*. I said I could make nothing of it, and was about to lay down my pencil when he said: "There is something more—*sdrawkcab-daer*"—he spelled out rapidly, and I took it down. It was quite unintelligible to me, so I thought no more about it, as shortly afterwards Sloan went into trance, and, besides others who spoke, was one claiming to be Huxley, who informed me, amongst other things, that the scientific group was present.

After the sitting I referred to the jumble of letters I had taken down, and found that by reading backwards it was quite sensible. "*I am Rayleigh read backwards.*" There is nothing evidential in all this, but Lord Rayleigh was a well-known scientist, a former President of the Royal Society and of the Society for Psychical Research, and might be one of the group of scientists Huxley said was present. Now Sloan spelled Rayleigh to me in his letter as *Raleigh*, and, after the sitting, on asking him how he spelled Rayleigh, he did so the same way. He said he had never heard of Lord Rayleigh, and never knew a name was spelled Rayleigh. The rapid way he spelled out the message backwards was remarkable. On enquiring afterwards I found that Sloan's description of the quiet man beside me tallied with that of the late Lord Rayleigh.

This is an interesting though not an evidential case, and I only mention it as such. All that happened could quite easily be explained normally. By enquiry, Rayleigh's appearance and manner could have been found out, in fact I remember reading in the *Daily Telegraph*, about a month prior to this incident, some remarks by Sir William Barrett on Lord Rayleigh in which the reporter described him as "a quiet man". Believing as I do that Sloan is honest, I personally do not give this as the explanation, and further, it would require a very retentive memory to remember a string of unconnected letters, and this Sloan has not, his memory being particularly bad.

I think I have now given sufficient to let one see how it is I have separated, or analysed, the informationI havereceived. A sI have said, eighty-three separate voices have spoken to me or to my friends. I have obtained one hundred and eighty "A1" separate items of information, and one hundred "A2" separate items of information, much of which was not known to me at the time, but which I verified afterwards as correct. Only one item I have not verified, because I have not been able to, and only one has not been substantially correct.

These evidential items of information are quite apart from the communications given in Chapters XI, XII, and XIII, entitled "Nights of Instruction," which, though both instructive and interesting, cannot be considered as evidence. Evidence in Psychical Research, to be of value, must contain information which it is impossible for the medium to have known, and the best of all evidence is information unknown to the medium and the recipient which is afterwards found to be correct. Much of what is recorded in this and the previous two chapters, and also in the chapter which follows, can legitimately be claimed as coming under this category.

CHAPTER X

STILL MORE EVIDENCE

"Is anything of God's contriving endangered by inquiry? Was it the system of the universe or the monks that trembled at the telescope of Galileo? Did the circulation of the firmament stop in terror because Newton laid his daring finger on its pulse?"—LOWELL.

In the foregoing pages I have given a record of evidence I myself have experienced, but what was just as convincing was the evidence obtained by others who went with me, at times anonymously.

Mr. McCully,[1] of Glasgow, has kindly given me permission to mention his name and record a few of his experiences. Mr. McCully is a shrewd, level-headed business man, and has only come by degrees to believe in the reality of the phenomena, through having obtained evidence, which he cannot explain otherwise than by the fact that the information he received came from his friends who had died but still lived, and remembered their time on earth.

I could give numerous experiences which other friends of mine have had, but to do so would run my record into several volumes. I shall therefore conclude these chapters of evidence by giving, some cases which Mr. McCully has written out himself in his own handwriting, and vouched for by his own signature.

Mr. McCully has had eighteeen years' close association with Sloan, and his experiences have been many

---

[1] I gave his address in the earlier editions of this book, but, as he was troubled by callers and letters inquiring for Sloan's address, I must omit it in this and future editions at his especial request.

and varied. When I asked him to give me some of these, he replied that his difficulty was to select those cases which could be considered most evidential, as he has received so much evidence throughout all these years. However, he selected four experiences, and what follows on this and the next four pages was written by him and not by me.

One of the most vivid and impressive messages I have ever received was from a young brother, Johnny by name; he had passed over suddenly at the age of twelve years. He was the youngest of the family, and of course the apple of his mother's eye. Shortly after his death she went to Australia. Every letter from my other brothers in Australia told me of her grief and despondency. Well, Johnny came through to me at one of Sloan's séances. After establishing his identity, I asked him if he knew where his mother was? "Yes," he replied, "I have just left her, she is in a big ship sitting on deck taking tea." Through my mind flashed the thought, "Is Mother coming home?" and this mental question must have been read by him as he continued: "No, I do not think so, but write and tell her not to grieve so much, her grief makes me unhappy, and I cannot be happy whilst she is so unhappy."

Well, to me the message was not understandable. I could not understand what my mother was doing on a big ship if she were not coming home, but at any rate I wrote out Johnny's message and sent it on to Perth, in Western Australia. A week or two later a letter came telling me that a brother had, in an attempt to lift her despondency, bought his mother a ticket for a first-class trip round Australia, and that

she was then on her way to visit a daughter in Sydney.
When in Sydney, the daughter took her mother to a
medium, where she got the same message from Johnny
in the same words, namely, not to grieve so much as
it made him so unhappy.

Some time afterwards, on leaving my house
going to business in the morning, I met the postman.
He knew I was always looking for letters from France
as I had three brothers serving. He handed me an
envelope, and, when I opened it, it contained a cable
that mother had died. I decided to tell nobody and
wait and see what would happen. I had not seen Mr.
Sloan for about three months, but that afternoon I
received word that he had a sitting that evening. I
attended, and at the séance there were three or four
ministers in the circle, and many voices spoke to them.
One especially seemed to be holding a reception of all
his passed-over congregation, names and addresses
being correctly given.

Towards the end, I caught the medium by the
hand, and, addressing the control, said: "Come
Whitie, have you never a word for an old friend?"
He replied: "Go away, Cully chief, I don't want to
speak to you." I said, "Oh, what have I done?" but
he persisted, "I don't want to speak to you." I still
held the medium's hand, and Mrs. Sloan, who was
clairvoyant, said: "Don't torment him, he does not
want to tell you." But I still persisted, and then she
said: "There is a lady who has been standing behind
your chair all night." Whitie then said: "I am sorry,
Cully, but it is your mother." I said: "It's all right,
Whitie, I was expecting her; has she anything to say
to me?" Immediately the trumpet rose and a whisper

came: "Sandy, Sandy, I want to give you a message from your father. He wants you to write to his people. He is not pleased with you." This was a complete thunderbolt. I had quarrelled with my father's people over money matters; it had happened years previously. I had not given it a thought for years. No one in that room, I am certain, knew my affairs, and it was just such a message as he would send, no more, no less.

Towards the end of the war I had a visitor, a young soldier from Perth in Australia. I took him up to Sloan's one night, and to him came a voice giving a name and regiment, but he said: "Sorry, but I do not know you." The voice replied: "You will find my name on the war memorial in Perth." "I don't know any war memorial in Perth," my friend replied; "where is it?" "It is in —— Avenue" (the name was given but I have forgotten it). "Well," my friend said, "I know Perth pretty well, but I do not know any Avenue of that name." A year later I got a letter from him saying, that during his absence a new Avenue had been opened, under that name, into the park, and on the triangle there had been erected a memorial, the name of the man being engraved on it, just as he had been told at the séance.

On another occasion an artist friend was away painting a picture, in connection with the raising of funds for a memorial. He was the guest of the local Provost or Magistrate. This dignitary had lost a son in the war, and my friend, in conversation, had told him of the wonderful messages coming through the mediumship of Mr. Sloan. The gentleman was very anxious for a sitting, and my friend arranged with me to bring him and his wife to one. I was a little late in meeting them, and in consequence the usual introductions were dispensed with, so that when we got into the house I was a little confused, and had completely forgotten his name, and could not introduce him to the medium, who just laughed and said: "Any friend of Mr. McCully is welcome."

I found out afterwards Sloan's impression was that the gentleman did not want his name mentioned. However, the sitting had not long commenced when the medium, now under the control of Whitie, rose from his chair, and, walking over to the stranger, said: **"Your son says you have something upon you that belongs to him."** The gentleman said "Watch? pocket book?" etc., to which the answers were: "No, no." Then the medium started stroking the man's shoulder, and Whitie said: **"Your son is stroking your jacket."** "Yes," said the gentleman, "I have my son's suit on."

The conversation went on, evidence piling on evidence, and, going over to the mother, the voice, speaking through the trumpet, said, **"Do you remember, mother, the footprints on the linoleum? I caught it for that."** It appeared that, whilst on his last leave, he wanted to take his sister skating. The mother objected, as the sister had a cold. However, when the family had retired, the brother and sister had gone off to the ice. On their return the sister had taken off her shoes, and her feet, being wet, had left footprints on the polished linoleum, which the mother spotted in the morning.

After the termination of the war, a lady came to see me, with very strong family introductions. Could

I take her to a séance, she asked me repeatedly, but the difficulty was that there were so many anxious to get in and so few vacancies, as only three or four new people could be introduced each night, and every member of the circle had friends anxious to get in. However, it was arranged, and, accompanied by my wife and myself, the lady was introduced. The anxiety of the lady was caused by the fact that her brother, who had been at the war, was reported missing and could not be traced. When the sitting commenced her brother was not long in coming through, and told of his death. As he described it, he was blown to bits.

Later on another voice came through saying his name was Cameron. Both my wife and myself knew a lad named Cameron who had been killed, and, as no one in the circle claimed him, we said he might be a friend of ours, but the trumpet kept over by the visitor and persisted he was for her, but she denied all knowledge of any one named Cameron. The voice said he had served with her brother, but he had been taken prisoner and died in Germany. Of course it had to be taken as said, but the sequel was that our friend, some time later, got a letter from people named Cameron, saying they had heard that she was enquiring through foreign agencies about her brother, and would she be good enough to ask about their son who had been serving, and was posted missing at the same time as her brother. Evidently this was the Cameron who spoke to our friend along with her brother, all unknown to her that her brother had a friend of this name.

This concludes Mr. McCully's report.

Any enquirer, who wishes to pursue this subject of evidence further, will find 435 pages of Vice-Admiral Usborne Moore's book, entitled *The Voices*, devoted to it. This is a record of his, and other people's experiences with the well-known direct voice medium Mrs. Wriedt.

I have, in the previous chapters, given information purporting to come from voices, either through the trumpet, or apart altogether from the trumpet. Sloan, however, is one of the finest trance mediums in the country, and sometimes a communicator, if he cannot get his message through correctly by direct means, controls the medium or sends the message through one of Sloan's regular controls.

I have had messages given partly one way and partly the other. However, for long continued conversation, trance communications are the best, as they are more sustained, uninterrupted conversations lasting often for over an hour. In this way I have received much detailed information as to how the Direct Voice is produced, what the etheric body really is, the conditions existing in the world beyond, and the relative structure of the substance of which that world is composed, as compared with our physical matter. A stenographer present has recorded what was said.

First of all I am told that the whole universe is made up of substance of various degrees of density and vibratory activity, that this fills all space, in which life exists in varying degrees of development. What we sense here on earth is only matter vibrating within certain fixed limits. Surrounding, interpenetrating, attached to, and moving with our earth, is another world of etheric matter in a higher state of vibration. Consequently it is unperceived by our senses. In our physical world the real, or enduring, body is an etheric body, which, at the moment of our conception, commences to gather round it, or, in other words, clothes itself with physical matter slow in vibration. The etheric body is the framework on to which physical matter is attached. This etheric body is composed of substance quite in tune with the etheric matter of the next plane, but so long as it is attached to physical matter it is limited by the limitations of such matter.

At death, however, the etheric body is released from its physical covering, and continues functioning quite naturally in the etheric world, where everything is as real to it as it was when in the physical. The etheric body is, in every particular, a duplicate of our physical body, and so it can be understood how, if conditions are given for an etherian to re-materialise his organs of speech, it is possible to vibrate again our atmosphere and make his voice heard. The mind which controls the etheric duplicate carries over with it, I am told, everything but the physical covering. Character, memory, affection, personality, etc., go with the mind, because they relate to the mind and not to the physical body. The etheric world is, in many respects, similar to this world. Our senses there respond as they do here, but, owing to the finer structure of etheric substance, the mind can work on it in a way it cannot do here. Hence it is in this sense a mental world, but our present world is also a mental world as I tried to show in Chapter III.

In this next state of consciousness, the inhabitants

find themselves in surroundings much the same as we experience here. There grow trees and flowers, but there is no death such as we understand it, all vegetable life, instead of decaying, dematerialises and disappears from sight. The surroundings of the inhabitants are greatly conditioned by their thoughts, and so their houses and mode of life are much their own making. This, I am told, does not constitute the next state to be one purely of mental projections, because its inhabitants have the same sensations as we have, as they can feel, touch and smell the flowers, they can gather them, and, when walking in the fields, they meet and talk with their friends.

All on the same plane, I am told, can see and touch the same things. This is the reply I invariably received, when trying to find out whether this state was objective or subjective. There are many planes, but only those on the same plane experience the same sensations. I have, myself, experienced etherians present who talked to me, but they could not see each other, though they were in the same room, the explanation given being that they were in different planes of existence. These etherians are men and women, not vaporous spirits, but real, vital and tangible people, such as we mix with every day. Theirs is not a dream world, but one of objective reality, intensely real—everything, music, art, and all constructive work being at a higher pitch than we can possibly understand.

Great activity prevails, and everyone has his or her own work to do. Service to others, and fellowship, are the ethical standards which prevail there to a higher degree than here. There is a universal language;

each and everyone can understand the other. It is inherent. Nationalities generally live together and speak their own language, but there is one language common to all. My informants were insistent on the point that with them discipline was rigid, and all had to obey those in authority. Everyone is under the authority of higher etherians, whose laws and instructions must be carefully obeyed. It is a well ordered and well governed state.

There is no night as we understand it, and the light they get does not come from our sun. If they want rest they can get subdued light, but not darkness as we experience it. When asked as to their food, I was told that they ate and drank just as we did, and enjoyed the same sensations, but their eating and drinking were different from what we understand by these words. They enjoy much more freedom of movement, as they get from place to place at a speed we cannot comprehend. On other occasions, when I put questions about the composition of our minds, I was told that mind was substance in a very rapid state of vibration, and that at death, though we left on earth our physical brain, yet the mind in etheric life functioned through the etheric duplicate of the brain which survived death along with the rest of the etheric body.

All life persists. Animals as well as human beings survive death, and each enters into a state harmonious to the vibrations of each. Affection on the part of an animal for an individual can bring the two together again after death, but, without this bond of affection, they would function unsensed by each other in their own plane. Thus, life is indestructible, a great universal force is everywhere, in everything, in some form or another, but only when in conjunction with the physical can it be perceived by our limited sense perceptions.

Physical science deals with physical matter, something we can sense. Psychical science deals with etheric matter. We cannot sense etheric matter, but etherians can. Its atomic structure, I am told, differs from that of our matter. It may be ether, or something akin to ether, for all we know to the contrary. Physics and psychics are twin brothers, which makes it easier for a physicist to understand psychics than scientists in other branches of knowledge. Hence the whole tendency of physical science to-day is towards the view, that not physical but etheric substance is the basic structure of the universe.

Only the ignorant affirm that just what we sense is real, that beyond this range of sense nothing exists. Our range of sense, our sight, our touch, our smell and hearing are limited to the last degree. We know that the spectrum of the spectroscope proves the very limited range of our ordinary vision, and that further ranges of vibrations of what might be colour, could we see them, extend on either side. It has been said that the perceived vibrations, as compared with the unperceived, are much less than an inch is to a mile. Therefore, it is evident that there lies an enormous region for other life to inhabit around and within this world of ours, a region quite beyond our normal sense perceptions.

Until one clearly understands that our senses here only respond to a very limited range of vibrations, what we term physical matter, that outside these there is a universe full of life which responds to a higher range of vibrations, unreal to us, but more real to it than physical matter, one cannot grasp or understand in all its fulness the psychical phenomena which develop through mediumship.

CHAPTER XI

NIGHTS OF INSTRUCTION

"Our object in life should be to accumulate a great number of grand questions to be asked, and resolved in eternity—Now we ask the sage, the genius, the philosopher, the divine, but none can tell; but we will open our queries to other respondents—we will ask angels, redeemed spirits, and God."—FOSTER.

AFTER I became convinced, not only of the medium's honesty, but also of the identity of those who purported to communicate, I was naturally anxious to know something of their mode of living, their surroundings, and how it was possible for them to return to earth and make their voices heard. In the four previous chapters I have summarised some of the information I have been given, which proved to me the identity of those who spoke. In this, and the next two chapters, I shall confine myself to three sittings I had, when the questions I put, and the answers I received to my inquiries, referred to their life and surroundings and their mode of communication. The information with which I deal is from notes taken down at the time by my stenographer, and is typical of those sittings I had for the purpose, not of seeking tests as to identity, but information regarding the etheric world about and around us.

These nights of instruction were particularly valuable and impressive, as, except for my stenographer, I was alone with the medium. I had, therefore, the opportunity to put questions, and receive replies, without the feeling that I was in any way monopolising those in the etheric world who had come to meet and speak to others besides myself. At ordinary séances, the more there were of us the greater was the evidence, especially when strangers were present.

On those occasions all my attention was given to proving identity, and that those who spoke were really those they purported to be, but in these times I had alone with Sloan my mind was directed more to receiving instruction and general information. Then it was that my etheric friends, though present, kept silent, and allowed others to speak who had greater knowledge than they had yet attained. On these occasions some voices spoke to me which I did not recognise, and no acquaintanceship was claimed; they were cultivated and had a command of language far beyond the capacity of the medium.

In this, and the other two chapters which follow, I shall report three sittings, the first in December 1923, and the other two in January 1924. They are representative of a series of private sittings extending over a year.

At the December sitting my informant spoke in slow and measured tones, without a trace of accent; his delivery was impressive, and, although I could not see him, I visualised a man of dignified carriage, culture and education addressing me. Sloan, as usual on such occasions, was in deep trance, his hands held in mine, his head fallen down over his chest, and, except for various twitchings from time to time, he sat motionless. I sat facing him, Miss Millar, my stenographer, on my right at the table taking notes,[1]

---

[1] Miss Millar used a note-book with embossed lines, made for the purpose of taking down shorthand in the dark.

and except for the three of us there was no one belonging to this world in the room, or for that matter in the house, as Sloan at this time was living alone. As a precaution, however, I locked the room door and put the key in my pocket.

Miss Millar, moreover, is decidedly mediumistic, and this contributed in no small measure to the success of these private sittings, as the combination of her psychic powers with those of Sloan made conditions almost perfect.

This first séance I am now reporting took place on 4th December 1923, at 7 p.m., and a few minutes after taking our seats and putting out the light this strange male voice spoke to me as follows:—"Mr. Findlay, the last time you sat with my medium you expressed the desire for information relating to our world. I have been requested by those who are responsible for what takes place here, to come to-night to help you in any way within my power. If you will ask me what you wish to know I shall do my best to answer."

This voice spoke from high up above my head. I was sitting facing Sloan, my hands holding his, my feet touching his feet. As it spoke I leaned forward to make certain it did not proceed from his lips, but there was not a sound nor a whisper. Ventriloquism could not account for it, as any ventriloquist will testify that this form of deception is impossible in the dark.

I thanked the speaker for his kindness in coming, and the conversation proceeded in the form of question and answer, each reply being instant.

Question: Here on earth we can only appreciate

the physical, namely, the earth, the sun and stars. What is contained in what we call space?

Answer: I can only answer you so far as my knowledge permits me. Interpenetrating your world is another world of substance in a higher state of vibration to the one you sense. The universe is one stupendous whole, but you only appreciate what you see and hear and feel. Believe me, there are other worlds of substance, finer than physical matter, in which life exists and of which you on earth can form no conception. Connected with your earth is this world to which I came after what you call death. Encircling your world are planes of different density, and these move in rotation with the rotation of the earth.

Question: Is your world, then, a real and tangible world?

Answer: Yes, it is very real to us, but the conditions in which we find ourselves depend on the condition of our mind. If we wish it we can be surrounded by beautiful country. Our mind plays a large part in our life here. Just as we live in surroundings suitable to our mental development, so we also attract to ourselves minds of the same type as our own. Like attracts like in this world. So also like attracts like so far as your world and our world are concerned. The evil-minded here are attracted by the evil-minded in your world, and the good here by the good with you. We can, at will, take on earth conditions by lowering our vibrations. Our bodies become heavier and more perceptible to the human eye, which accounts for our being seen at times by those who have the faculty on earth of sensing our vibrations.

Question: Do all the inhabitants of your world get into contact with the earth from time to time?

Answer: The higher and more developed we become the less are we in touch with your world. The more development proceeds the less do we think of the earth. It is all a question of desire. We can come into contact with earth conditions at will; if the will for doing so is absent then we do not return to you.

Question: Do we always retain our individuality?

Answer: Think of a country-side with glens and hills. The rain falls, and gradually trickles down into small streams, which streams gather volume until they enter a brook, which brook in turn enters a river, which in turn enters a larger river and sweeps onward to the sea. Each individual can be compared to an atom in the raindrop. The atom retains form and individuality throughout the whole course, from the hill to the sea, and even in the sea it does not lose its individuality. So with us, we move onwards and onwards, always retaining our individuality until we merge into the sea of full understanding, when we become part of the Divinity.

Question: That is certainly a very clear illustration, but to go back for a moment to the reply you gave me in answer to my question about your world being tangible and real. You stated that your surroundings depended on the condition of your minds. Now is your life purely a mental one, or can you touch and feel your surroundings just as we do here? In other words, is your world a material world like ours?

Answer: Our world is not material, but it is real for all that, it is tangible, composed of substance in a much higher state of vibration than the matter which makes up your world. Our minds can, therefore, play upon it in a different way than yours can on the material of your world. As our mind is, so is our state. To the good their surroundings are beautiful, to the bad the reverse.

Question: Do you mean that you live in a dream world where everything appears real but is not?

Answer: No, we do not live in a dream world. As I have said, we live in a real tangible world, though the atoms composing it differ from the atoms which made up your world. Our minds can act on this tangible substance in a way yours cannot do on your world. You live in a world of slower vibrations.

Question: Does each of you, therefore, live in a world of your own?

Answer: Everyone does, you do and so do I, but if you mean can each of us see and feel the same things, I answer, Yes. All in the same plane can sense the same things. We have the same world as you have, but in a finer state.

Question: Can you touch what you see?

Answer: Yes, of course we can touch and feel and enjoy all the sensations you do.

Question: Do you eat and enjoy your food?

Answer: Yes, we eat and drink, but it is not what you mean by eating and drinking. To us it is a mental condition. We enjoy it mentally, not bodily as you do.

Question: I cannot see you, but, if I could, what would you look like?

Answer: I have a body which is a duplicate of what I had on earth, the same hands, legs and feet, and they move the same as yours do. This etheric body I had on earth interpenetrated the physical body. The etheric is the real body and an exact duplicate of our earth body. At death we just emerge from our flesh covering and continue our life in the etheric world, functioning by means of the etheric body just as we functioned on earth in the physical body. This etheric body is just as substantial to us now, as the physical body was to us when we lived on earth. We have the same sensations. When we touch an object we can feel it, when we look at something we can see it. Though our bodies are not material, as you understand the word, yet they have form and feature and expression. We move from place to place as you do, but much more quickly than you can.

Question: What is the mind? Is it something apart from the brain?

Answer: Certainly it is. You bring your mind over here with you. You leave your physical brain on earth. Our mind here acts on our etheric brain and through it on our etheric body, just as your physical brain acts on your physical body.

Question: Will you tell me something about your world?

Answer: All in the same plane can see and touch the same things. If we look at a field, it is a field to all who look at it. Everything is the same to those in the same condition of mental development. It is not a dream. Everything is real to us. We can sit down together and enjoy each other's company just as you can on earth. We have books and we can read them. We have the same feelings as you have. We can have a long walk in the country, and meet a friend whom we have not seen for a long time. We all smell the same aroma of the flowers and the fields as you do. We gather the flowers as you do. All is tangible, but in a higher degree of beauty than anything on earth. Here we have no decay in flower or field as you have. Vegetable life just stops growing and disappears. It dematerialises. There is a similarity here to what you call death. We call it transition. In time, as we develop sufficiently, we pass on to another plane from which it is not so easy to come back to earth. This we call the second death. Those who have passed through the second death can come back and visit us in our plane, but we cannot go to them until we have passed through it also. This is what your Bible calls the second death. Those who have passed through it do not often come and speak to you on earth directly by materialising, as I am doing now; but they can pass their messages on to me, or someone in my plane, and we pass them on to you.

Question: You told me your world revolved with this world. How does this happen, and also, do you travel with the earth round the sun?

Answer: The spheres nearest the earth do so because we belong to this planet. We cannot see your world revolving in space, because we revolve with you. We cannot see your world until we take on earth conditions. In taking these on, we slow down our vibrations, and come through from one plane to another, until we get our vibrations down more to a level with those of which your world is composed. We can all come down, but we cannot go up beyond our own plane until we are prepared for the change.

Question: What would happen to you if this earth came into collision with another star or planet and was destroyed?

Answer: It would make no difference to us, our world is quite independent of physical matter.

Question: Do we re-incarnate again on earth?

Answer: Now that is a question I find difficulty in answering. I have known no one who has. I passed over many years ago, and I have round about me those who lived thousands of years ago on earth. That is all I can say, because my knowledge does not permit me to say more.

Question: Do dogs, cats, and other animals survive death?

Answer: Yes, sir, most emphatically yes, they do survive. No life becomes extinct, but they do not survive in the spirit world, as we term it. They have a spirit world of their own making. They do not exist in a spirit world as man exists. If, however, say a dog has affection for a human being it can get into his or her surroundings if both have left your earth.

Question: Is your vegetation similar to ours?

Answer: Something similar, but much more beautiful.

Question: I have noticed in my many conversations with different people, that those who had titles on earth never give them, only just their christian and surnames. Sir William Barrett, for instance, asked me to drop the "Sir" when speaking to him.

Answer: Yes, that is correct. Earth titles mean nothing to us. As soon as those bearing them arrive here these prefixes are dropped, they are meaningless to us.

Question: What are your houses like?

Answer: Our houses are just as we care to make them. Your earth houses first were conceived in your mind, and then physical matter was put together to make them as your mind first saw them. Here we have the power to mould etheric matter as we think. So our houses are also the products of our minds. We think and we construct. It is a question of thought vibration, and so long as we retain these vibrations we can hold the object, which during this time is objective to our senses.

Question: What languages do you speak?

Answer: There are the various earth languages spoken here, such as English, French and German, but they are conveyed from mind to mind mentally. Communication takes place mentally from one to another, not only by the spoken word as on earth. This is just as if I were to say that the mind of the spirit gets into telepathic touch with the mind with which he is communicating.

Question: One last question; the power, I notice, is failing. Where do you get your light from and when do you sleep?

Answer: If we feel we want rest we can get subdued light; not so subdued as you understand it, but sufficient to enable us to rest. We have no night here as you would understand night. We get our light from the source of all light, but I cannot continue further to-night as the power has gone, so good-night, and may the Light that lightens all darkness lead you into the light you are so earnestly seeking.[1]

---

[1] At a later date much information was given to me on this subject, and this will be found in *The Unfolding Universe*.

I expressed my gratitude for my unknown friend's kindness, and hoped that we might continue the talk on a future occasion.

The gas was relit, and in about five minutes Sloan came out of trance, and asked if anyone had spoken. As usual he was dazed, and lay down on the sofa for a few minutes while Miss Millar made him some tea, which quickly restored him. By the time we were ready to leave he was quite himself again, and said he felt no ill effects.

I was privileged to have these private sittings from time to time during 1923 and 1924, but the foregoing record relating to conditions in the etheric world must suffice, as I should like to give a report of two other private sittings when my enquiries centred on the means they adopted to make their voices heard on earth. What I have been told is summarised in previous chapters, but the phenomena are of such interest that I am sure the answers to my questions will be of interest to many.

I think I was as much interested in hearing how communication was established, as I was about the conditions governing the other world. I am no more anxious to leave this earth than is any other healthy-minded person. What I was glad to know was that death did not close the book of my life, and that the brief span from the cradle to the grave did not constitute the sum total of an individual's existence. So long as we are limited to the physical, the physical to all healthy people must be the main thing. Those who know me will admit that this every-day world of ours occupies every minute of my time. I am no dreamer or mystic. I am not psychic, and my

mind runs on practical every-day lines. Why, therefore, it may be asked, have I taken so much trouble
to get into touch with another order of existence?

The answer is that I have an enquiring mind. To
most people one séance with Sloan convinces them
of the reality of the after life, and, unless they have
recently-departed relations with whom they wish to
keep in touch, that satisfies them. I, however, felt
differently. At the first séance I was not convinced,
but I was sufficiently impressed to wish to enquire
further as to the meaning of it all. I therefore returned
on the first opportunity after my first experience,
only to be more mystified than ever. However, I
was not going to be beaten. If it were all one huge
fraud I would find it out; if not, then I would have to
recast my whole outlook on life and death.

By taking elaborate precautions, and devising
ingenious tests, I became convinced in time that the
phenomena were genuine, but I was not convinced
that the voices belonged to those who had passed
through death. Only gradually did conviction come,
and this was due to the knowledge the voices had of
things which no one present could possibly have
known, and only the one who claimed to own the voice
could have known. The voice which claimed to be
my father's, for instance, showed such knowledge of
our family life, of our home, and of my business,
which was his before his death, that the only thing
lacking was that I could not see him. If I could,
there would have been nothing else necessary to
complete conviction.

We cannot call a person "dead" who returns to
us in a body similar to the one he had on earth, and

talks to us as he did when here in the body. Several independent people with clairvoyant power, who had never known or seen him on earth, described his appearance so accurately that at last I became convinced that I was in reality talking to my father, as, if it were not he, who was it? In earth-life his physical appearance and personality represented to me my father. Here it was all repeated, and not with him only but with dozens of others whom I had known on earth.

Further information I have obtained is to the effect that the real world contains seven spheres, besides the earth, interpenetrating each other. Each has a plane or a surface, and an atmosphere which appears as sky to its inhabitants. Looking upwards here on earth we are looking through these, and the same on each plane, they look through the ones above. The surface of each sphere is solid to its inhabitants, but, by thought, they can lower their vibrations and come through from plane to plane right back to earth. How few of us realise, when gazing towards the sky, that we are looking through planes of different density, which some day will be our home, and where those who once lived on earth are experiencing an active and useful existence.

The next chapter will continue the records of my enquiry, an experience which I shall always look back upon as Nights of Instruction.

CHAPTER XII

NIGHTS OF INSTRUCTION (Continued)

"How pure at heart and sound in head,
With what divine affections bold
Should be the man whose thought would hold
An hour's communion with the dead."—Tennyson.

THESE nights of instruction aroused in my mind the wish for more and more information. If there were such a world as they claimed to be living in, I wanted to know something about it. I had all the enthusiasm of an explorer on the frontier of an unexplored country. I wanted to know what it was like, what it felt like getting there, and what I should do here to make my position as comfortable and happy as possible when I got there.

After I got this information, my thirst for knowledge was not fully satisfied. I then wanted to know how it was they were able to speak, how etheric substance, which is intangible to us, could vibrate the atmosphere. I felt I was up against the most important scientific problem it had ever been the lot of man to fathom, and I was determined to get a thorough explanation of the subject while the opportunity for doing so occurred. I therefore made use of some of these private sittings for this purpose. The following then, is a record of a sitting I had on 4th January 1924, when Miss Millar, Sloan and myself were the only people in the house. The door was locked by me, and the key remained in my pocket until the sitting concluded. No one could possibly be hidden in the room as I always made sure of that.

We took our seats, Sloan facing me, Miss Millar on my right, with her note-book and pencil, and after about ten minutes Sloan began to twitch. The trance state then came quickly, and his usual control White-feather spoke. We talked to each other for a few minutes, and then I asked if conditions were good. "Yes," Whitefeather replied. "Very good, lady got great power and this helps us. Lots of people here to-night, the monkey man here too." This curious remark referred to the etherian who said he was known on earth as Professor Huxley, whose talks to me by the Direct Voice on evolution earned for him this title by that amusing, witty, but rather ignorant individual who goes by the name of Whitefeather, and who, according to his own account, as I have previously stated, was once a Red Indian Chief.

"I want to hear how it is that they speak by the Direct Voice, Whitie," I said.

"Me can't you you much, Findlay Chief" (the name he always called me). "But Greentree here to-night, he will tell you."

I had spoken often before to Greentree. He also claimed to have been an Indian chief on earth, but he was a very different type from Whitefeather. He told me on one occasion that he had learned English after he had left the earth, because in etheric life he had been much in touch with English-speaking people. His English is good, not broken English like White-feather's, who had picked up what he knew through controlling the medium. Whitefeather's case is similar to others I have experienced, the control being quite ignorant of our language when first taking possession of the medium's body, and learning it gradually through hearing it spoken. Greentree's superior mental and cultural development was always apparent, and Whitefeather, while acknowledging his own inferiority, spoke of Greentree at all times in terms of respect. He would say, when unable to answer a question: "Greentree will tell you, Findlay Chief, if you ask him the next time he speaks."

It may be asked why it is that American Indians sometimes act as controls of our mediums. I put the question once to Greentree, and was told that this was because in earth life they were Spiritualists, and were in constant touch with departed spirits. They had learned on earth the laws governing communication between the two worlds, and, when they themselves passed into the etheric world, it came more easily to them than to others to get into touch with earth again. Just as certain people on earth are fitted by nature to act as mediums between this world and the next, so I have come to realise that some etheric people are likewise more adaptable than others for controlling a medium. We therefore find that all trance mediums have one or more regular controls, who speak more easily than others through the medium's own vocal organs. These are the mediums on the other side. Not everyone can communicate by controlling the medium, and this is done by those best fitted for the work, who pass messages, received by them from etheric people, on to earth.

Control of the medium may be more difficult than speaking by the Direct Voice, and I have found that most of my friends who spoke with their own voices, quite apart from the medium, became proficient after a little practice. The one advantage Trance Speaking has over the Direct Voice is that it can be sustained for a long time, sometimes for an hour or more, whereas by means of the Direct Voice long-sustained speech is unusual. After a few minutes the voice trails away and becomes inaudible, and we have to wait, sometimes for five minutes, before it again gathers the power to speak.

All the same, while the power lasts, the Direct Voice is much more effective and impressive, because, however short the conversation, a "face to face" talk is always to be preferred to one by means of a control. For instance, we would be more impressed if, let us say, a foreigner spoke for a few minutes to us in English, and then waited some time to think what next he would say, rather than express himself by means of an interpreter. By direct speech he conveys his thoughts to us in a way he cannot do if everything he says has to be passed through, and expressed by, a second person.

Greentree is one of Sloan's regular controls, and he speaks through him with ease, but besides this he is very proficient in speaking by the Direct Voice. He is also one of the chief operators on the other side. It will be remembered that in Chapter VI, when describing how the voice was produced, I stated that the greater part of the work done to obtain speech between the two worlds was carried through by those on the other side. Greentree is the director of the séance, both on his side and ours, he is in charge and directs those wishing to speak, explaining to them how this can be accomplished. He singles out those who are to speak, as, with the large number waiting an opportunity, direction is required. He controls both sides, and does not hesitate to tell us on this side, and sometimes pointedly, if we are not making the right conditions. He tells us when music is required, if we are too tense, and he reprimands someone for sitting with his legs crossed, a habit which is one of the first things a novice at a séance is told not to practice.[1]

The novice, thinking that no one will see him in the dark, sometimes disobeys this injunction, but forgets that the darkness is no darkness to them, and that they see clearly everything we do. A tap by the trumpet on the culprit's head, and a polite request not to cross his legs, invariably proves this; in fact I have never known a mistake to be made. The usual enquiry as to how they knew gets a quick answer from Greentree, which makes the novice realise that normal conditions do not rule at a séance, and that intelligences are present with powers beyond our own. Other instances have occurred, quite apart from the regular voice phenomena, to show that the etherians present can see in the dark. I shall mention a few.

At the close of a sitting, just before the farewells are said, I have often held out my watch and asked the time, and on every occasion, when the lights have been turned on, I have found the reply to be correct almost to the minute, and this, be it remembered, is done in the dark and when no luminous watches are in use. This correct time telling, moreover, occurs after a sitting of from two to three hours. Again,

---

[1] The reason for this is to keep all the orifices of the body open, as it is through them the ectoplasm is drawn.

if I hold my finger in any direction, it will, on request, be gently touched with the trumpet; no fumbling, a clean gentle touch. Any part of the body, on request, will be cleanly and gently touched, either the right or left ear, the nose, or the right or left knee, an impossible thing, as I have proved, for any human being to do in the dark.

This brings me to an incident which occurred, just after Whitefeather had informed me that Greentree was waiting to speak. Miss Millar had put the light out, and I was holding Sloan's hands and controlling his feet. We had both been sitting a few minutes in the darkness waiting for Greentree's voice to speak, when Miss Millar said, "My notebook is being moved about," and then, "It has been taken away from me," followed by, "My pencil has been taken out of my hand". Then the table, nearly two yards away from the medium, rocked up and down with considerable force. I replied, "It cannot be either Sloan or I doing it, as my feet are touching his and my hands have a grip of his hands", when a voice up near the ceiling spoke as follows: "**Just something to make you understand that there are intelligences at work in this room to-night which can see you and the things in the room. What is the dark to you is not darkness to us. A materialised spirit hand is responsible for what has happened, but the lady need have no fear, we never would do anything to frighten or hurt anyone.**" After this the notebook and the pencil were returned to Miss Millar, the table stopped rocking, and Greentree spoke, wishing us "**Good evening**" and asked me what I wished to know.

Question: How is it that you can speak to us on earth?

Answer: By materialising my etheric mouth and tongue.

Question: Can you tell me something of the method by which this is done?

Answer: I shall do my best to make you understand how this is done, but remember you cannot get a proper grasp of the difficulties we are faced with until you yourself come across to our side. However, I shall explain our methods as clearly as possible. From the medium, and those present, a chemist in the etheric world withdraws certain ingredients which for want of a better name is called ectoplasm. To this the chemist adds ingredients of his own making. When these are mixed together a substance is formed which enables the chemist to materialise his hands. He then, with his materialised hands, constructs a mask resembling the mouth and tongue. The spirit wishing to speak places his face into this mask and finds it clings to him, it gathers round his mouth, tongue and throat. At first, difficulty is experienced in moving this heavier material, but by practice this becomes easy. The etheric organs have once again become clothed in matter resembling physical matter, and, by the passage of air through them, your atmosphere can be vibrated, and you hear his voice.

Question: But how do you get this air? Are the lungs also materialised?

Answer: In a full materialisation, yes.

Question: I have often heard two, or sometimes three, voices speak at once. Are other masks used in these circumstances?

Answer: Yes, on these occasions conditions are good, and the chemist has sufficient ectoplasm to construct several masks, which are all sometimes used at the same time. That accounts for your hearing more than one voice speaking.

Question: Where is this mask placed?

Answer: Usually in the centre of the circle. The chemist keeps as much ectoplasm as possible within the circle, but, when the quantity given off by the medium and sitters is small, it gathers about the floor, which accounts for voices coming from the floor when conditions are poor. On the other hand, when conditions are good and we have an ample supply, we can build right up to the ceiling, which accounts for the voices on these occasions coming from high up in the room.

Question: After the mask is completed, what do you do?

Answer: The person wishing to speak takes up his position in the centre of the circle, and presses into the ectoplasmic materialisation and then commences to speak, moving his mouth and tongue just as you do when you speak.

Question: What about the trumpet?

Answer: This is used, not only to magnify the voice, but to enable it to be directed towards the person we wish to speak to. The trumpet is moved by materialised rods, and is controlled by one on this side whom we term the trumpet operator. His name is Gallacher, and he will speak to you now. (A new voice spoke, announcing himself as Gallacher, the trumpet operator.)

Question: Good evening, I take it that you are Irish.

Answer: Yes, sir, right first time.

Question: Well, my friend, I want to know all you can tell me about your work in helping those on your side to speak to us on earth.

Answer: When a spirit wishes to speak to you he takes on earth conditions from your surroundings. We always know when your meetings take place. (Here Whitefeather broke in "It's me who knows, and I tell him and the others. It's me who knows when a meeting is to take place, it's me that remembers these things, it's written down; it's me that tells everyone.") After this interruption Gallacher continued: As I was saying, we always know when you are meeting. I am responsible for manipulating the trumpet. I have been standing beside you waiting to speak to you, and I am glad of the chance to tell you what I can.

Question: So you are reponsible for the megaphones or trumpets?

Answer: Yes, I deal with them entirely. When there is going to be a meeting, the chemist whom I work with generally lets me know when it is going to occur, and asks me to come along at the specified time. He supplies a substance, and also obtains a certain amount from the medium and the other sitters. It is the combination of this spirit-substance with ectoplasm, drawn from the medium and sitters, which enables us to materialise. If there is enough it allows the metallic instrument to go to all parts of the room, and voices to be produced. When I came to-night I first looked to see where I could best gather the most ectoplasm. The chemist gets it from me and adds his ingredients, and it is then conveyed to the most suitable place. I also speak for those who cannot do so, and also for those who may be a long distance away. These latter send me their messages as you send messages by wireless; these are picked up by a receiver and given to me; I then pass them on, giving the person's name. I merely act as an Exchange.

Question: Does that account for what is sometimes thought to be impersonation?

Answer: I am the one who passes the message through, but you may sometimes think that I am not the right person speaking. I am the messenger to you from those who cannot speak.

Question: I am glad of that explanation, not that I have ever experienced impersonation, but it is interesting and helps me to understand your difficulties. Now can you tell me anything more?

Answer: When spirits come into the circle to speak they actually, for the time being, partially materialise; their mouth and tongue being coated by the substance we make. There is a nexus between the medium's larynx and the materialised mouth and tongue of the spirit speaking, which enables the words the speaker forms to be heard by you. We then feel as we did when on earth. The organs of speech take on a thicker form, our tongue thickens and so do all the other materialised organs. We cannot be heard by you until we again put on matter of slower vibration, and it is only when we find someone like the medium, who can supply us with this ectoplasm, which we fashion to our requirements, that we can again make you hear us. Ectoplasm alone, however, would be of no use without the chemical substance we supply from our side. It would not materialise without it.

Question: What is this substance?

Answer: The chemist is standing beside me, and tells me to say it is no use giving you its ingredients as they would mean nothing to you on earth. He says, however, that the finished product is a substance by which material things can be moved. Nothing can be moved without it. All physical bodies are composed of many different ingredients from which we draw the substance you call ectoplasm.

Question: Can you tell me anything more?

Answer: I must go now, but before going I would like to tell you, sir, that I was brought up in the Roman Catholic faith, but I did not come over here as a Roman Catholic. Before coming here I gave up all creeds. I came here a free thinker, but I was wrong in not believing in survival. I came here minus my physical body. When I keep in touch with the earth plane my surroundings are practically on a par with the physical world, but in the higher spheres we get away from earth conditions. Now I have for the time being taken on earth conditions, and I am part of your world. I will touch you (I felt a touch on my left arm) and I am conscious of that touch. (Sloan's hands and feet were still controlled by me. If Miss Millar had touched me she would have required to stop writing, get up and come over to me, but her pencil never ceased moving, and, when I told her immediately I was touched, she answered from her correct place in the room.) Many of us here in our normal state often touch our friends on earth, and at first are much distressed that no notice is taken of us, forgetting that with our more refined bodies we cannot be seen or felt. I must go now; good-bye! Greentree will speak to you again.

Question: I once put my ear right up to the medium's mouth when a voice was speaking, and heard a hissing sound. My father's voice was speaking at the far end of the circle to my brother, yet no words came from the medium's lips, only a soft hissing sound. At other times, when I have done the same thing when a voice was speaking, I have heard nothing. What was that hissing sound I heard?

Answer: From the medium's mouth is projected a materialised ectoplasmic tube to carry the vibrations of his larynx to the spirit speaking. The medium's larynx is used to vibrate the atmosphere, the spirit's materialised mouth, throat and tongue to form the words. You were fortunate to hear this hissing. Your scientific men interested in the phenomena would have been glad to have had your experience, as it is something to give you a start in getting some real knowledge of how the voice is produced.

Question: Can you tell me something more about the mask which you enter when you wish to speak?

Answer: You can call it a mask or a dummy. We gather the ectoplasm from the sitters into what I might term an urn; not a physical urn. If you wait a moment I shall try and show you it. (Sloan's hands and feet were still controlled. I waited, and gradually there appeared high above his head a luminous object which assumed the shape of a large flower-pot, and then faded away.) Did you see it? (Yes, I replied.)

Well, we gather the ectoplasm into this, and the chemist adds his ingredients. The finished product is matter slow enough in vibration to vibrate your atmosphere. The mask, until it is entered by the spirit wishing to speak, is incapable of speaking itself. The spirit has to tune down his organs of speech, and thus contact between these and the mask becomes established. When the magnetic or psychic power is strong enough, there is no difficulty in obtaining sufficient cohesion between the speaker's organs and the mask. When cohesion is established, the ectoplasmic material moves with the vocal organs of the spirit. It is exactly as if we coated our mouth and tongue with this material. It sticks to them and moves with them.

Question: Has this mask weight; would it affect a balance?

Answer: Yes, it has. The ectoplasm taken from the sitters has weight, and the sitters' weight is reduced in proportion to the amount that is withdrawn. If you were to sit on a weighing-machine during the sitting you would find your weight decrease. The ectoplasm is returned to the sitters at the end of the séance and they become normal. [This has been proved correct by experiment.]

Question: When you control the medium and use his vocal organs, what really happens? [This refers to trance utterances, not the Direct Voice.]

Answer: When the medium is controlled, and we wish to speak through his vocal organs, we get him into a passive condition. This is the condition he is in when in trance. His spirit has left his body for the time being, and is outside. When he is in this condition we are able to work on his larynx and vocal cords, his tongue and throat muscles. We do not go inside him, however, but stand behind him. We are able to get ourselves into a condition, or in tune with the medium, to such an extent that when we move our voice organs the medium's move likewise. There is a connecting link, etheric or psychic, whichever you like to call it, which has the same action on the medium's muscles as a tuning fork on another tuning fork if they are both tuned to the same pitch. Thus the two sets of vocal organs work in harmony. There is no question of the messages in any way being influenced by the medium's mind, as his mind does not come into the question at all. We do not work through his mind, but directly on his vocal organs. Everything that comes through is exactly as it originates in the mind of the controlling spirit. The medium's mind and brain are switched off for the time being, and the spirit operator controls the muscles of the medium's vocal organs.

Question: The medium is still in trance; where has his spirit been since we started?

Answer: When the trance state comes on it means that the medium's spirit has moved out of his body. His spirit is at present exactly on his right not far from his body.

Question: Can you tell me more of your controlling the medium during trance?

Answer: I take on earth conditions, slow down my vibrations and stand behind him. Ectoplasm is found everywhere in the human body. When I stand behind him it is similar to standing behind the mask, only in this case it is the medium's own vocal organs which I move to form the words; they move in company with my organs; whereas when we speak directly, apart from the medium, we enter the mask and form the words by our own tongues which are temporarily materialised.

At this point in the proceedings Sloan stood straight up, his arms outstretched, and I did so with him. Thus we stood facing each other. Greentree then said he had broken off the talk to show me something. "I will show you that his spirit is out of his body. Both your arms are stretched apart, as you still hold his hands. Now try to lower his arms." I tried, but they were as stiff as if he were a wooden image. I felt his muscles, and right down his body, every part of him was like wood. "Rigor mortis," a voice shouted, and indeed it was. With all my strength I could not move one arm or the other either up or down. I gave up as I felt that if I exerted too much pressure his arm would break. Then another voice: "We shall bring his spirit back and take him out of trance." Gradually the muscles slackened and I placed him gently down in his seat. In a few minutes Sloan's voice spoke, asking if we had had a good sitting.

Sloan is not so tall or muscular as I am, but, on the first chance I got, I asked a man more muscular than I am to stand up, with his arms outstretched, and keep them rigid while I tried to pull them down. I had not the least difficulty in doing so, and my readers can make the experiment for themselves. Evidently, to give me further proof on this occasion, Greentree withdrew Sloan's etheric body further away from his physical body, so that for the time being he was as one dead. In ordinary trance the etheric and the physical must be in closer connection, as there never is this rigidity of muscles. It was an experiment I am glad was not often repeated, as only on one other occasion did I have a similar experience.

I shall conclude these Nights of Instruction in the chapter which follows.

CHAPTER XIII

NIGHTS OF INSTRUCTION (Concluded)

"The wise are instructed by reason; ordinary minds by experience; the stupid by necessity; the brutes by instinct."—CICERO.

THE only other record I shall give of these private sittings is the one dated 24th January 1924. Miss Millar again acted as note-taker, and I held Sloan's hands, my feet always touching his. At each sitting similar conditions ruled. Sloan sat opposite me, and in about ten minutes went off into trance. The light was put out, and we waited in the darkness wondering what further we would learn this night.

"Good evening, Mr. Findlay." "Oh, good evening, Greentree," I replied, "I recognise your voice."

Question: I am glad you have come to-night. Now can you tell me the difference between trance and sleep?

Answer: In sleep—that is, natural sleep, the sleep the physical body needs—all the functions of the body are at rest except the heart, which keeps on pulsating. That is natural sleep, but the spirit does not always leave the body. In trance we put the spirit slightly aside, but a psychic cord is attached to his body from his spirit-body. If that cord should be snapped, dissolution would take place immediately. Before we can speak through him we require to get his spirit out of him, outside altogether, but it is still attached to the body by this cord of life. He is now unconscious and outside his physical body. His spirit at the moment is exactly between his body and you. If nothing untoward happens he can return to his body

166

just as he left it. If something should go wrong in his present condition, the physical frame suffers. On this occasion you will notice I am speaking to you by means of his vocal organs. I am standing behind him, but am in such close contact with these organs that, just as I move my mouth, his mouth moves. I am in complete control of these organs. The medium knows nothing, he is quite unconscious of anything I do. I am taking temporary use of his body, as the power is not yet strong enough to speak to you by the Direct Voice.

Question: Can you hear me quite easily?

Answer: Yes, I can hear you, but I cannot hear what I say in reply. I am talking behind the medium and I suppose you can hear me.

Question: Oh yes, I can hear you all right. Can you suggest a means of communication without a medium?

Answer: By finding something on earth susceptible to the higher vibrations of the spirit world. This, scientists on our side are trying to influence you to accomplish, as it is a thing for you to do, not us. We cannot do more than get our vibrations down to near those of your earth. It is for you to get your vibrations up to meet ours when we come down.

Question: How does a medium hear clairaudiently?

Answer: By our acting on his mind.

Question: What will my work be when I reach your world?

Answer: You will be eminently suited for research work.

Question: When you speak to us, do you lower your vibrations?

Answer: Certainly, that is what we mean when we say we take on earth conditions.

Question: How is it you lower your vibrations?

Answer: It is difficult to explain. It is a condition you get yourself into, which enables you to absorb the ectoplasm from the medium and sitters, and when I do so I feel just as I did when I lived on earth.

Question: How do you hear us speak?

Answer: By lowering our vibrations sufficiently to catch the atmospheric vibrations of your voice. I must go now. Good night.

After a few minutes a new voice spoke. "Green-tree has to go, he has other work to do; but he has asked me to speak to you in case you have anything more to say.

Question: Thank you for coming. You might tell me how it is you are able to speak to me. Green-tree and Gallacher and others have told me, but the more information I get the better I can understand your methods. So far everything I have been told by different voices harmonises and agrees. You go on talking. You may say something I have not heard before.

Answer: I feel as if I were just back on earth again. This is just as interesting to me as it would be for you to come over here to our side and see how this is worked. You would be fascinated seeing all that takes place before a spirit voice can vibrate your atmosphere. First we are told by Whitefeather, or someone else, when a séance is to take place; he is always about the medium and knows everything he does, and hears when he arranges a séance. Then we all come. Whitefeather gets the spirit-body out of the medium's body, the chemist and his assistants come with their preparations, and Gallacher comes to manage the trumpets—not that the trumpets are always necessary; you have often heard us speak without them. They just magnify the voice and enable us to throw it more easily to the person we wish to speak to. Greentree takes charge and tells the spirits present how and when to speak. It is very interesting watching all the arrangements being made on this side, the chemist linking up the medium and sitters, and drawing power from them. Until all these preparations are completed no voice can be produced that you could hear. The larger end of the megaphone or trumpet is also used to place the materialised mouth and tongue in, as it gives the spirit speaking something to rest them on. Then we speak, pointing the smaller end to the person addressed.

Question: Is Gallacher here to-night? I want to ask him something.

Answer: (Whitefeather interposed.) No, Gallacher is busy at other work. He cannot come to-night. He told me you were coming, me tells them when to come, that's my work. Me look after my medium's spirit. Away people, who will do you no good. When you come as an earnest enquirer you will find us ready to help you. [This was addressed to some Etherians present.] Our band here won't allow bad spirits to come here. Me can get right into medium's body, but no one else can; me manage this after years of practice.

It is impossible in a book to convey to the reader the different tones and personalities of the speakers. Whitefeather is recognised at once by his voice, his personality and his speech. Whenever he speaks you want to laugh, he is like the clown at a circus, sometimes he sulks, sometimes he is, figuratively speaking, as black as thunder, only to brighten later and become, by a little flattery, all sunshine. By his quaint remarks and sallies he can keep us laughing for minutes on end. He butts in and twits the Etherians speaking, or makes some remark about a sitter—altogether a very amusing and interesting personality, but one by no means highly developed. Likewise with all the other regular speakers, they are easily recognised, each has his own characteristics and personality which the darkness of the séance room cannot hide.

To continue the conversation interrupted by White-feather:

Question: Do you keep records of what takes place?

Answer: Yes, of course we do; we are not encyclopedic.

Question: How is the trumpet moved?

Answer: When the power is strong enough the spirit's hand is sufficiently materialized to enable him to hold it, but on other occasions by psychic rods. (A pause.) Someone near you is very anxious to speak; just wait and don't ask any more questions. [Then I received two quick taps on my right shoulder, and I knew at once my father was beside me because he was the only person who ever tapped my shoulder like that. It was a familiar action peculiar to him, as he would slip up to a friend and give the back of his shoulder two quick taps with his fingers. Then he spoke to me, and the rest of the sitting was taken up speaking to him and other friends who were present.]

Huxley, to whom I have already referred, also spoke, tracing matter and life from early beginnings, through the physical, into the etheric world. "Evolution," he concluded, "is still my great theme, the thing I am constantly thinking about. Evolution is the key to the Universe. Evolution never ends. We are always progressing, progressing, but we retain our individuality. It helps to explain the mystery of existence."

I have done my best in these last three chapters to give an outline of the methods I employed to get information relating to the other world about us, and to find how it was its inhabitants were able to communicate their thoughts to earth. These private sittings were very impressive, and did as much as anything to convince me of the reality of the other world. Sitting face to face with Sloan, and, when a Direct Voice was speaking, pressing forward to make certain the voice was not his, confirmed the conclusions I had previously formed, and these, as I have already stated, were not arrived at hastily.

I felt that I had now a double check on all I had previously experienced; I had confirmed the medium's honesty; the super-normal nature of the phenomena; the reality of another world in close proximity to our own; and lastly the continuity of life, which I found had only passed beyond our knowledge owing to its having discarded the physical garment which appealed to our senses. Besides this I had been told something of the life and work in the etheric world, and of their methods of establishing communication with this earth. Truly these nights of instruction were not to be forgotten.

CHAPTER XIV

ADD TO YOUR FAITH, KNOWLEDGE

"Ignorance is the curse of God; knowledge is the wing wherewith we fly to Heaven."—SHAKESPEARE.

THE foregoing chapters contain information which has seldom been conveyed between two different orders of intelligence in the same clear and concise way. Doubtless we were not ready to receive it, and had it come sooner it would not have been understood. To-day the position is different, as the younger generation is now able to think of the ether and its waves, and of matter composed of atoms and electrons. The human mind has thus advanced sufficiently to be able to grasp the fact that nothing is solid as we understand the word, and that everything we see and touch is composed of that substance called ether, which only when vibrating at a certain frequency appeals to our senses.

The vast majority of the vibrations of the ether never affect us, though we know by means of instruments that they exist and most likely have always existed. Is it inconceivable that there are other beings who can sense what we are incapable of sensing, or is the sum total of intelligence confined to what we call humanity? Is there no other life capable of appreciating ether waves, either below or above our limited capacity? Surely to adopt this view reveals a very limited outlook. We know how primitive man was able to appreciate only his own immediate surroundings, and how he regarded the stars as lights placed in the firmament for his special benefit. His mind could not have grasped the discoveries of Copernicus.

Had Bacon in 1623, in his *De Augmentis Scientiarum*, discoursed on the vibratory activity of matter, his work might have died at birth. The human mind in his day could hardly comprehend the majesty and greatness of the physical universe, and the universe of ether could only be appreciated when first of all the physical universe was properly understood. This mental development took three hundred years, and to-day we find just the same difficulty in harmonising ourselves with this next forward step, as did our fore-fathers in adjusting their minds to the astronomy of Copernicus and Galileo, and, in later years, to the biology of Darwin.

Each forward step takes time; the great minds take the first step, often amid jeers; but by-and-by the multitude follows. Our children will be able to appreciate the etheric universe in a way many of the older generation never will, because to them an etheric world beyond the physical will be comprehensible as it will never be to their parents and grandparents.

It required at least one hundred years before the discoveries of Galileo and Copernicus gained general acceptance amongst educated people. Then, just as now, appearances were different from reality. It took fifty years and more, after Darwin, before most of the educated were able to accept the fact that our earth, and its inhabitants, are the outcome of a slow but steady evolution and not an instantaneous creation. All new discoveries have had to meet with uncompromising opposition. History is full of the fact that humanity has invariably persecuted, and sometimes murdered, its greatest thinkers, and afterwards worshipped at their graves. The human mind is so constituted that new ideas penetrate slowly, and are only accepted after long and fierce discussion.

No doubt this conservatism is for the best, as, if it were otherwise, there would be no stability, whereas, though truth always wins through in the end, much chaff is discarded in the winnowing. Every radical change in science, religion, or philosophy has only won its way to acceptance by ultimately appealing to the reason of mankind, and psychic discoveries will be no exception. We must therefore expect that it will take time before this new knowledge becomes part of the generally accepted truths of the world, and this will only come about by more and more earnest seekers investigating the phenomena, and year by year accumulating further evidence which in the end will remove all doubt.

What, therefore, must be the attitude of all those who, putting aside prejudice, set their faces earnestly towards the truth? What should be my attitude under the circumstances so far related in this book? Should I keep silent, or tell the world of my discoveries, ignoring its jeers and scoffs? Each one of us is but the trustee of knowledge entrusted to him, and to hold back for fear of ridicule would be but cowardice.

I tell only what I have been told, and this book is not the product of my imagination. I am not a missionary trying to change beliefs long held. I am only relating something I have heard and seen, which will make more intelligible those beliefs held sacred by the great majority of mankind. If, in the process of assimilating further knowledge of the unseen, certain beliefs now held as fundamental are found to be but symbols of a greater truth lying further back, is this not just a repetition of what has occurred in the past?

Knowledge is like a tree of slow growth. Year after year it sheds its leaves which have been the means of its nourishment, but still the tree remains, slowly but surely adding to its stature and girth. So to-day certain old beliefs, which helped mankind onwards in his reaching out after God and the unseen, must be discarded so that place may be found for those of newer and fresher growth, but the real and enduring fabric will always remain. The knowledge gained by this new science of Psychics only confirms and deepens the great and universal truths proclaimed by Religion and Philosophy. We find in our researches an all-directing Mind, fashioning and moulding the universe, one great stupendous plan, far beyond the comprehension of anyone in this world and of most in the next. We find that as we sow here we shall reap hereafter; that we are making our next life in this; that life persists and is indestructible; that memory, personality and character are our real selves, and that it is not they but only their physical covering that decays at death.

Further, we find that we are surrounded by an unseen multitude who, under certain conditions, can hold converse with us from time to time. Have not the fundamental and essential truths of religion received confirmation by this new revelation, and are we more likely to become irreligious by its acceptance? When we look round at the so-called religious world of thought to-day, is there not an instinctive feeling, amongst even the most orthodox, that things are out of gear? Consider the sects, the dissensions and the quibblings on the one hand, and the utter indifference on the other, and we have the results of orthodox religion in a nut-shell.

If we take Britain alone as an example, we have just become sufficiently educated to make the majority of us wonder what is truth. In the old days of ignorance there was no difficulty in accepting truth, because truth for the multitude was what was told them by the Church. That was during the Dark Ages, but the printing press had its effect, and a few hundred years ago some were sufficiently intelligent to doubt the authority of this Church. They threw it over, and pinned their faith on what was considered an infallible book instead of on an infallible Church.

Knowledge progressed, the infallible book began to be doubted, and then more doubted, and, in consequence, since the Reformation, there has been dissension everywhere amongst the Protestant section of the community because they had nothing solid on which to base their beliefs. The Roman Catholic Church alone has managed to pursue its even way, without at least open disruption, but the history of Protestantism reminds one of an iceberg, forever breaking up. Each section, of course, considered itself right and the rest all wrong, and each section had its own texts to support its contentions.

To-day, nearly a third of the way through the twentieth century, we find the same form of Church service, the same rigmarole of words used which satisfied our ignorant forefathers, but they are far from satisfying the thinking section of the population. In consequence church congregations are becoming smaller, because people have little sympathy with its teaching. Are the people, however, indifferent to the essential truths which all religions have proclaimed? By no means, as many people to-day are more interested and fully alive to the essential truths of religion than ever before, and the Church has lost a great opportunity by retaining its impossible creeds, and thus forcing from it the thinking section of the population.

In the Church of England prayer-book there is set down to be read or sung, on certain Feast Days and Sundays, the creed of Saint Athanasius which tells us, among other things, that if we do not believe the incomprehensible we cannot be saved, and without doubt we shall perish everlastingly. This cruel creed sets out the Christian faith; it has never been repudiated or withdrawn; in fact it is the basis of Protestant and Roman Catholic Christianity, or, as the Prayer Book says, it is the confession of Christian faith. How can any intelligent man or woman read this creed and say honestly that this jumble of meaningless words constitutes his or her faith, and yet it is glibly sung or read throughout England on certain appointed Sundays.

The utter lack of authority, and basis for belief in Protestant Christianity, finds ample confirmation in the diverse opinions held with regard to transubstantiation. The Bishop of Birmingham (*Morning Post*, 23rd July 1931) accuses the Archbishop of Canterbury of countenancing the belief "that a priest, by the act of consecration, can cause Christ to come and dwell within the bread and wine of Holy Communion, and that the belief that a Spiritual Presence can be made to inhere in a piece of bread by consecration is false".

This is only an example of what has been happening off and on for the last 1,900 years. If it was not a discussion or an argument about transubstantiation, or the Trinity, it was a quarrel over the authenticity of some passage in Scripture. Christianity, since its foundation, has been the cause of one discussion and argument after another, relating either to creeds or forms and ceremonies on the one hand, or the meaning and interpretation of certain portions of Scripture on the other. Christianity has been like a ship at sea forever seeking a port and never finding one, because it has no sound and solid foundation for its assertions.

They have been dependent on the pronouncement of some Church authority, or some passage in Scripture, and these have received different interpretations in different ages. Consequently the Christianity of to-day is as unlike as possible the Christianity of the first century.[1] These opinions and interpretations have caused an untold number of divergent views throughout Christendom, and been the cause of the hundreds of sects which have formed the Christian Church since its foundation. Small wonder that only a small section of the community attends Divine service, because the leaders themselves cannot agree as to what is truth, and so their followers, losing heart, get fewer and fewer. The number of those attending

---

[1] The present beliefs of orthodox Christianity were not formulated till the year 325 at the Council of Nicæa. Prior to that date they did not constitute what is now termed the Christian Faith.

Spiritualist services, on the other hand, is yearly increasing.

What ray of hope is held out to those around an open grave? This is what the mourners are told: "We shall not all sleep, but we shall all be changed, in a moment, in the twinkling of an eye, at the last trump, for the trumpet shall sound, and the dead shall be raised incorruptible, and we shall be changed." Now to be changed is the last thing any one of us wants. Every one wants to be himself or herself, and retain his or her own individuality and personality, and this is just what we shall do in a body similar to our earth body. What comfort can my quotation bring to the sorrowing mourners, and yet at every Christian funeral the clergy read this obsolete burial service, or, if Dissenters, repeat similar words, and consign the dead to the grave until the great Resurrection.

This consigning of the dead to the grave until some future Resurrection day has been going on now since the commencement of Christianity; it went on before Christianity was thought of, and, if the clergy are right, our graveyards must be full of sleeping bodies awaiting the great roll call. In the past the people have accepted this old Egyptian belief in a bodily resurrection because they knew no better, but sooner or later, owing to our increased knowledge, the truth must become known. Anyone who doubts the foregoing view of the Church's opinion on the subject, will find it confirmed by reading over the well-known hymns which are sung at so many funerals: *Now the labourer's task is o'er* and *On the Resurrection morning.*

We cannot expect the clergy to repudiate the beliefs from which they earn their livelihood, and it now rests with Spiritualists to affirm that the essential truths of religion can be believed, not as an act of faith, but as scientific facts. I am told, however, that all that is new can be read into the old creeds, and that these dead bones can be made to live again by pouring the oil of the new revelation upon them. That may satisfy some, but it does not satisfy many who are now thinking for themselves, and passing over with indifference the pronouncements of the Church. These old writings are interesting relics of a by-gone age, but why ponder over the gropings of our ignorant ancestors after truth when we have before us these things they were seeking after?

What, then, is our position to-day? We now know that our survival and our entering into the etheric world is not conditioned by any kind of belief. It is a natural process, just as natural as birth; it takes place, not at some far distant future date, but at death. It does not matter in the least whether one believes in events recorded in the Bible or not, or whether one is a believer, on the one hand, that Heaven is a new Jerusalem with its streets paved with gold, or, on the other hand, that there is no such thing as survival and that the grave is our end.

All these beliefs mean nothing so far as survival is concerned, as the most ignorant believer, and the most pronounced atheist, will reach the etheric world when the time comes for his etheric body to leave his physical body. There is no separate place, Heaven for the believers or Hell for the unbelievers. But ignorance is not bliss and it breeds false imaginings.

The more you know of the country you are going to, and the means of entry, the more at home you will feel in it when you arrive there. We shall be much more in harmony with our surroundings if we prepare ourselves correctly in advance, though it is unwise to give too much thought to it.

I am writing with some authority, as I have had one or two interesting experiences. A clergyman who had died, told me that he could make no progress until the last of his congregation had arrived from this world. I asked him why, and he said that the reason was because he had preached to them orthodox Christianity, namely, the forgiveness of sins through the belief in Christ's death on the cross, and the punishment of all who had not this belief. He was waiting to tell each one of his congregation, as they came over, that he was wrong, and that he had given them an entirely wrong impression of the after life.

I was once told that all young children who had passed into the etheric world as infants, without any knowledge of this earth's religious dogmas and creeds, grew up quite ignorant of these, as these earth-made beliefs meant nothing to the inhabitants of that world. Those passing over, holding such beliefs, are taught to see their error, and those who have not preached them very quickly forget them in their new surroundings. Those, however, responsible for preaching and teaching error may have to endure mental remorse until they have forgotten their mistake.

Another experience I had was equally interesting, and shows how wide is the divergence of thought, wherever it be. The group, which was working along with me on the other side, said they were going to bring to speak to me a Plymouth Brother, who on earth had his ideas so fixed that he could not get rid of them in his new surroundings. This man, who I found out afterwards had been a prominent Plymouth Brother in Glasgow, being noted for his very narrow and bigoted views, and who had recently died, spoke much as he must have spoken on earth on many occasions. Talk about a hardened sinner! He was certainly the most hardened *believer* that I have ever experienced. From the other side he discoursed to me about the wickedness of everybody except himself. To him everybody was a sinner, and his fixed ideas on earth had been carried over with him. After he had finished I was told by the next who spoke that he would have to undergo a special course of teaching, and that in time his mind would develop sufficiently to enable him to see the truth.

As I say, the main essentials of all true religion remain. This new revelation takes nothing from the desires of mankind, and adds enormously to our knowledge of both this world and the next. We are all gainers by these new truths and we lose nothing. Let us therefore live true, upright, good and unselfish lives, remembering that it is not believing creeds that matters but what we are and do. No repeating of creeds or prayers will give us any better a place hereafter, as, though such repetitions give a measure of comfort, they do not make us better men and women. What is essential is the development of our character, and this is not strengthened if we are afraid to think for ourselves, and use either creeds or a book or a church as crutches, when we have sufficient knowledge before us to-day to enable us to walk alone.

In all my communications with those who have passed on, when touching on those deeper problems, I have been impressed by their insistence on the reality of their world, and how they look on this world of ours as but a poor imitation of theirs. The etheric is the basis of all life and to the etheric will it return. What we see is temporal, and it is the unseen that is eternal, as the seen and tangible are but the results of invisible causes. In nature nothing is lost. Life may cease to manifest in a physical garb, but neither life nor its covering is lost. Life pursues its course entering and passing through matter, which, during its passage, it endows with form and movement. When this covering ceases to fulfil its requirements, life leaves it to die and decay, returning it to mother earth, whence it came, so that it may be used again for the passage of life at some future date. Life but gathers within this physical covering so as to enable it to assume form, and in the more highly developed creatures this form persists in the etheric world. This earth is just an incubator, developing life during its passage through the physical; it is but the nursery of the human race, its place of preparation for the real and enduring world which is to us, in the physical body, both intangible and unsensed.

The great law which governs this etheric world is that of harmony, or the law of attraction, similar to our law of gravitation. As the physical body is subject to the latter, so the etheric is subject to the former. There, like attracts like, and, on arrival in the new environment, I am told that we are irresistibly drawn into that company and condition for which we are fitted by character. Congenial souls keep together, but progress is always possible even for the worst if the desire is strong enough. All can ultimately progress, if they wish to, though the way for the selfish is lonely and dreary. Our thoughts and actions, therefore, here on earth are building for us our place in the hereafter. How many of us realise that thoughts are lasting things, that they pass on with us through death, and will be our companions, to influence us in an even greater degree then than now. When separated from the physical body they assume shape and form more potent for good or evil than when clothed by the earthly body.

What I have stated in this chapter is based on the information I have been given by those who once, like us, lived here on earth. In many ways they have proved to me their identity, and, in ways I could prove, they have satisfied me of their honesty and truthfulness. Why, therefore, should I not also accept their statements of the kind of life they live, the appearance of their world, and their moral and philosophical teachings? They are one stage further on than we are, and see things from a new and larger angle. If what they tell me appeals to my reason, am I to discard it as of no value because the method of communication is not in general practice? Such an argument would have killed the telephone, the telegraph and wireless at their birth, as because of their novelty no messages would have been believed, and thus they would have been useless from the start.

Constant repetition, however, proved their value, just as the constant repetition of messages, which have been going on between the two worlds for the past eighty years, has confirmed in all essential details this great new revelation of a world about and around us, its life and its character. What has been told to me has been told to others, not once, but thousands of times. I am but adding another stone to the cairn, which some day will rise so high that all mankind will be forced to look upon it and believe.

CHAPTER XV

FACTS WE OUGHT TO KNOW

'Facts are to the mind, what food is to the body. On the due digestion of the former depend the strength and wisdom of the one, just as vigour and health depend on the other. The wisest in council, the ablest in debate, and the most agreeable companion in the commerce of human life, is that man who has assimilated to his understanding the greatest number of facts."—BURKE.

WE are all bound for another country. If we were told we would have to leave England and take up our permanent residence, let us say, in some little-known part of South America, how anxious we would be to meet someone who had been there. Would we not ply him with questions, not only about the scenery and the climate, but about the kind of clothes we should take with us?

When I had this opportunity with those who had returned to me from the etheric world, to which we all are travelling, I naturally took every opportunity to find out about this place, its inhabitants, its scenery and how best I could clothe my character so that I should be most suitably fitted for my new environment. Having thus learned something of our destiny, let me, in as simple terms as possible, set down these facts we ought each one of us to know. To those uninterested in the future life, to those who prefer to enter it ignorant and unprepared, this book will not appeal. All know that death must come, and those who wish to meet it with knowledge and understanding will find here food for thought.

Here in this world our bodies are dual; physical,

which we can see and touch; etheric, which we cannot sense with our physical organs. These two bodies interpenetrate each other, but the etheric is the permanent, enduring one, the etheric mind being the abode of our memory, personality, and all those qualities which make up our character. Those qualities pertain to the etheric. The mind never grows old, only the brain—the mind's instrument—which becomes impaired as the physical body grows old. Nothing we have learned, no intellectual wealth acquired, is ever lost.

Here we lose, in time, the power of expression; but this is due to the physical instrument ceasing to function with its aforetime precision. When, after the death change, the worn-out garment is laid aside, we stand, clothed in an etheric body, in our new abode. Freed from the limitations of the physical, our faculties are clearer and movements more rapid. In the change we lose nothing of value; we are still ourselves in form and feature, in thought and action. Those who have lost arms or legs will have them again, as it was only the physical which was lost, and the same with all the other bodily disabilities.[1] The physical is but the covering; it is continually wasting away and being renewed by the blood, which is another proof that there is a permanent structure to which physical matter is attached.

The child who leaves this earth as such grows to manhood or womanhood, and when this stage is reached remains a fully-grown developed man or

---

[1] The individual mind in the etheric world obtains in time such control over the etheric body that bodily deformities can be removed and cured by thought.

woman. Old age pertains to the physical, but it is unknown in the etheric. Children in the etheric world are carefully cared for and educated; there they have their schools and colleges; in fact the desire for knowledge is the outstanding desire of all who seek for progress, be they children or adults. And what of the old who die? Do they who live long enough to die with all the disabilities of old age retain these throughout eternity? If we could only comprehend that the etheric body never grows old, but only the physical body, this question would not be asked. When the old and tottering body is cast aside the etheric duplicate stands erect, freed from its outward physical handicap.

The old die old only in the physical sense, but enter the next life young. Age there is not measured in years, as time there differs from ours. We count our time by the revolution of a physical globe round a physical sun, but when we leave our earth we enter a new environment where time, such as we understand it, does not exist. Our only earthly experience of the relativity of time is during sleep. We then, in dreams, pass through experiences which, if awake, would take us years to accomplish, but when asleep they happen in a few minutes and sometimes in seconds.

I have been told by my instructors in Etheria about those who left this world a thousand years and more ago, who are only now beginning to appreciate their new surroundings. But such cases belong to those of low development in this world, who find it difficult to adjust themselves to their new conditions and environment. The man and woman of average intelligence perceives the new environment without much delay, some almost immediately, on the passing of their etheric bodies out of the physical covering, though with others it may take days or weeks, as we measure time.

Our etheric body is in every respect a duplicate of our physical body. This may seem strange at first, and I found it difficult to grasp until I understood the fact that the etheric is the real body on earth, and that from the moment of conception it has gathered round it physical matter, slow in vibration. Otherwise it could not have functioned in the physical world owing to its finer and more rapid vibrations.

The physical body is only a protective covering for the etheric during its passage through the earth life. In reality, our real hands here are etheric hands clothed with a glove of physical matter, and so with all the other parts of our body. Our real brain is the etheric brain, through which the mind functions, and it acts through this whether we are in this world or the next. The mind acts on the etheric brain, and the etheric brain on the material covering which we call the physical brain.

Those who have made the change called death can see our minds at work, and study our etheric brain working under the influence of mind in a way we cannot. They tell me that it is just like looking at a technicolor film, because the different vibrations which impinge on our eyes vibrate the mind, and it is these vibrations that we call sight and colour. These pictures formed by our mind can be seen by Etherians, and consequently everything we think can be read by them in the etheric world just as easily as we can read a book.

We are really much greater than we think we are, very much so; our mind as expressed through the physical brain is very limited, and only when freed from the physical do we comprehend its greatness. Our earthly mind we call conscious mind, but it, and what we term the subconscious or subliminal mind, form the complete mind. Our conscious mind directs our activities in this world, but our greater mind functions in the next. We obtain only glimpses of this greater mind in the occasionally observed phenomena of telepathy, clairvoyance, clairaudience and prevision, and on these occasions the subliminal over-rides the conscious for a limited time and then withdraws.

Some day, as man develops, the subliminal may become more and more a dominating factor, but at this stage of our development its intrusion is sporadic and confined to the few. When we pass on, our earth memories pass with us, but slowly they fade and we are guided and governed by this greater mind which has been with us all our lives building up our bodies, performing its inward functions, and making us what we are, though we know it not.

One other important fact has been impressed on me time and again by my informants, namely that the next is a very real world; no floating on some fleecy cloud in some disembodied state which has no form or feature. There we are men and women, just as we are here; the word Spirit is only an earth term, and a bad one because it is so misleading. Not only are our etheric bodies similar in every way to our earthly ones, but they are as solid, real and tangible to their owners as ours are to us. For instance, it may seem strange to be told by an inhabitant of this world of finer matter that he took pride in keeping his finger-nails polished; but, as he has finger-nails, why should he not be as careful of them as we are of our physical nails? Just because he has discarded the physical covering, his etheric nail becomes no less real. Let it be remembered that when we discard the physical it becomes the unreal, and the etheric the real to our consciousness.

We have much to learn concerning matter. It does not cease to exist when it becomes invisible to our physical eyes. This can be better understood by taking some water, heating it, and then observing the effect. First we have steam partially visible, then super-steam invisible. By reversing the process we can bring back the invisible super-steam to water. Though invisible, the super-steam is still matter. All we did was to increase its vibrations, and then reduce them until we had water again. Our etheric bodies vibrate at a frequency beyond the capacity of our physical eye to catch, but, under certain conditions, when freed from the physical body after death, these vibrations can be lowered, and, with what is called ectoplasm borrowed from the medium, the vocal organs can again vibrate our atmosphere in speech.

In recent years we have come to learn that space is not an empty void, but contains a substance we call ether. Here dwell the myriads of the so-called dead, in a world to them as material as is ours to us. This etheric world is the real world, as it forms the basis of everything we term physical. This etheric world is both a condition and a place. It encircles our earth as do the belts and zones around the planet Saturn, but it interpenetrates as well, as physical matter forms no part of this etheric world. Here we live within the limits of physical vibrations; there they live within the limits of the vibrations to which their etheric bodies are fitted.

Everything to them is as natural as our world is to us here; they have houses, schools, churches, fields, trees, flowers, music, clothes, and all the pleasures the mind desires. The family tie unites again those whom affection held together on earth. There is no working for money, and the absence of money is about the only thing different from this earth. Everything else socially is similar, as the same minds that were on earth are there and have the same ideals and ideas as they had here. There, however, they are living in a finer environment which they can mould in a manner impossible here on earth.

It is mental wealth that is sought after, as our thoughts condition our environment in this next plane of consciousness to a degree unrealised here. Those of low intelligence, and of evil thought, make their conditions low and evil, whereas those of pure and high thinking have the conditions suitable to their thoughts. Hence the importance of giving due regard to the development of our character on right lines here and now, as just as we leave the physical so shall we enter the etheric.

If we have no noble thoughts here we shall not have them there. If we go through this world like Bunyan's character, with a muck-rake in our hand, looking no way but downwards, we shall not be able to look upwards there. Only by undoing our errors will progress in time become possible. Why not, therefore, live here so that our progress onwards may be both steady and continuous? We are day by day making our future habitation; if our thoughts are pure we shall dwell with the pure, if evil then our abode will be with the evil.

It is therefore the duty of each one, individually, to live here on earth so that his next stage on the journey may be in truth a further step on the road to the fulness of wisdom which, however many the by-paths we traverse in error, we should, if we have the desire, reach in the end.

CHAPTER XVI

CONCLUSION

"To be perfectly just is an attribute of the divine nature; to be so to the utmost of our abilities is the glory of man."—ADDISON.

Now, I ask, what have we to make of it all? Have I been the victim of a great fraud, has all that I have recorded, and much else, a normal explanation? Is all I have been told about the next world a deliberate lie, or the outpourings of a highly imaginative mind? Have all the voices been Sloan's voice, and has he impersonated every individual who spoke? Has he some marvellous means of obtaining information about the deceased friends of those who come to his circle? Has he the power of knowing everyone, whether he has seen them before or not?

Can he see in the dark, and, though his hands and feet are controlled, can he, in the Séance Room of the Glasgow Society for Psychical Research, by some means, touch everyone ever so lightly about the face and hands with the trumpet, often using two trumpets at the same time? Has he some wonderful faculty of being able to read our thoughts in the dark, and answer our questions before we have spoken them? A few simple experiments proved that this is impossible. I need not ask a question aloud; my friends in the etheric world can read my question in my mind and answer it, or tell me what I am thinking about.

This often happens when I am not being spoken to. I may be sitting quietly awaiting a voice to speak, and thinking of something quite apart from my surroundings, and a voice will speak to me on the subject of my thoughts. This in itself is proof positive of a personality present with powers beyond those possessed by any physical being, and it occurring in the dark makes it all the more remarkable. It might be possible for a human being, with the deductive faculty of a Sherlock Holmes, to have some idea of our thoughts in daylight, from a study of our facial expressions, but in the dark, never.

Is Sloan really not in trance at all, but, besides manipulating the trumpets and impersonating voices through the trumpets, is he at the same time assuming different personalities himself, so that we have two personalities speaking which are none other than Sloan himself? I have heard thirty separate voices speaking during one séance, each of different tone and personality. Further, how can he describe so accurately the appearances of the etherians purporting to speak? Is it all one huge fraud, and have I and others been the victims of a great conspiracy? If it be so, it is quite the cleverest performance ever accomplished. Infinite trouble is necessary, and also considerable expense in gathering all the information, and for what purpose? Sloan's work takes him out at 7 a.m., and he does not get home until 6 p.m. When can he find time to make such exhaustive enquiries?

Except on the occasion referred to in Chapter IV he has never, to my knowledge, taken any money for all this time and effort on his part. Is he insane on this question, and for a morbid love of notoriety does he carry on this farce? If so, why so retiring, why so anxious at all times to hide his light under a bushel? Why does he not want to be introduced to those whom he calls "my grand friends"? Why does he prefer quietness and being alone to holding séances; and why, from time to time, does he sign on and go for months to sea where he never hears or speaks of Spiritualism?

I have asked myself a hundred questions from time to time, in my endeavour to find an explanation. Is it telepathy? If so how do you account for the Eric Saunders episode and dozens of others, and in any case how can telepathy produce a voice apart from the medium? Am I the victim of hallucinations? If so, my stenographer and all present are also the victims, and collective hallucination, going on for twenty years, as it has done with some of Sloan's friends, is unthinkable, as what *one* hears *all* hear at these séances. Often I have heard etherians speaking to, and answering each other during the séance.

What about cryptæsthesia—hidden memories, or the perception of realities by extra-sensorial channels? Can a memory, or the perception of realities by extra-sensorial means, produce a voice? Can my hidden memory, or his extra-sensorial perception, make Sloan able, normally or supernormally, not only to describe correctly my deceased friend, whom he never knew, but to produce also his voice, which I can recognise, which voice tells me things I had never heard before, but found afterwards to be true? Why, if this be so, do these manifestations concern only those who have passed on, the so-called dead? Again, why does someone in etheric life bring others to speak whom you and they knew on earth, and, at times, bring those whom you did not know were his friends, but afterwards found out were so? How can a medium know, normally or supernormally, not only your own friends who have passed on, but their friends also in Etheria, who were your friends and theirs in this world, or their friends only, quite unknown to you until confirmed by enquiry afterwards?

Nothing I can think of besides fraud or reality explains satisfactorily to me all that I have experienced. Fraud, knowing Sloan and the facts as I do, I rule out of account. The circumstantial evidence in favour of reality is overwhelming. No one has followed Sloan's actions and words, in trance and out of trance, more critically than I have done, and, all these years I have known him, never by word or action has he done or said anything to make me in the least degree suspicious as to his motives.

Sloan is a high-minded, upright, religious man, without much learning, and with average intelligence. A good workman, but no student. His range of literature is very limited. He told me once that he had seldom ever read a book in his life, owing to poor eyesight. I have never seen a book in his house, though I have been in every room of it, and only once an evening paper. He has not the capacity to carry on a séance, such as I have described, normally, for ten minutes, even if he wished to do so. I dislike referring to fraud in connection with a man of such high principles, but others do not know him as I do, and, to those who have not had the experiences which I have had, fraud is the simplest and the most obvious explanation.

I rule out fraud, I rule out telepathy, I rule out cryptæsthesia. I come back every time to the only explanation which fits in with all the facts, namely, that those we thought were dead are still alive; that they have bodies such as we have of a finer texture than our physical bodies; that they inhabit a world of finer matter than we do, and that certain individuals called mediums can supply them with a substance which, when mixed with ingredients of their own, enables them again, for a limited time, to assume physical conditions, and, with their memories, affections and character unimpaired, once more hold conversations with their friends still on earth.

My mind remains open for further explanations science may offer, but, so far, science has not given to me another explanation which fits in with all the evidence. In fact, science, until recently, has given little thought to the phenomena I have described. The London Society for Psychical Research has spent years studying mental phenomena, and this independent voice phenomena, equally if not more important in so far as personal identity is concerned, has never, to my knowledge, been officially investigated. It should be quite possible so to isolate the materialised mask that its weight could be taken and its construction and operation better understood. We must learn the laws governing the phenomena. There is a great field before the investigator, and I trust that what I have written will encourage someone with a scientific mind to pursue these investigations to a point which will make clear what to-day is obscure, as a thorough scientific grasp of the phenomena is essential.

The foregoing is a faithful record of my experiences, and I have but done my duty in recording them. Some may accept them, others suspend judgment, whilst many doubtless will disbelieve, arguing that without deception such things cannot occur. I reply to critics on much the same lines as did Pasteur to those who opposed his discoveries on *a priori* grounds: "In all this there is no question of religion, nor philosophy, nor atheism, nor materialism, nor spiritualism, it is entirely a question of fact." The facts are there, and refusing to face them does not alter them. If any one has built up a system of belief which opposes these facts, that system must be changed to suit the facts, because the facts will not alter to suit any particular system of belief. Science and Religion, on the acceptance of these facts, will, I believe, be united, and mankind will take an immense step forward in intellectual development, so much so that the human family will be united in a bond of harmonious brotherhood.

I can now safely leave the future to bring forth cumulative evidence in support of my assertions, so that the day will come when to disbelieve in the reality of psychic phenomena will be but to plead ignorance, and to scoff will be accounted foolish. Meantime the world is composed of those who do not think deeply on such subjects, or, if they do, are satisfied that there is nothing more to learn, and that all we can know of the universe is already known. On the other hand, there are others who have learned something of what exists beyond the veil from those who have gone before us, and, in consequence, have had their vision enlarged. As Mrs. Browning so aptly puts it:

> "Earth's crammed with Heaven
> And every common bush afire with God
> But only he who sees takes off his shoes."

John Campbell Sloan passed on peacefully on Thursday, 24th May, 1951, at the age of 82. For nearly fifty years he put his mediumship at the disposal of humanity without asking for reward or praise. Many have obtained an enlarged outlook, and received renewed hope and comfort, because he lived. In all humbleness and modesty he gave freely and expected nothing.

APPENDIX

188 FACTS GIVEN AT TWO CONSECUTIVE SITTINGS TO ARTHUR FINDLAY

My Mother died on the 3rd of February, 1936, and I think that the readers of *On the Edge of the Etheric* will be interested to read of her return shortly after her death. This occurred at two séances, one in Glasgow and one in London.

These two séances produced what I consider is first-class evidence, which came through the mediums when in trance and not by the Direct Voice. Not one mistake was made, everything was correct, some statements being unknown to me and found later to be correct. In both cases the mediums could not have made any inquiries beforehand, and I am quite satisfied that neither of them knew that my Mother had died.

Notes were taken at the time of the sittings.

Taking the sittings with the two mediums together, 188 facts were given to me which were correct. No mistakes were made and there was no guessing. Everything was said straight out. Nothing was vague. Everything said was correct and clearly stated. So that the reader may better understand this, I have put at the end of each paragraph the figures 1, 2 or 3, according to the number of correct statements given which could not have been known by the medium. When one correct statement is made the figure 1 is to be found at the end of the paragraph.

When two correct statements were made, the figure 2 and so on.

If the reader adds all these up, he will find that 188 correct statements were made at the sittings held on the 9th and 12th February, 1936, and that nothing said was wrong. So the record of these two sittings can be read right through from beginning to end without question.

SITTING WITH MRS. BERTHA HARRIS, IN GLASGOW, ON 9TH FEBRUARY, 1936

Mrs. Bertha Harris arrived in Glasgow from Chester on the evening of 8th February and went to the Holland Street Spiritualist Church, where she was given a bedroom and a sitting-room. My brother John and I, knowing that she was to be in Glasgow on the Sunday, 9th February, motored to Glasgow from Ayrshire and arrived at 11 o'clock in the morning. No previous appointment had been made, and we went up to Mrs. Harris's room and knocked and were asked to come in. I had only met Mrs. Harris once, some years earlier, after a meeting I addressed in Leicester, but she did not recognise me. She did remember John, my brother.

After the sitting with Mrs. Harris, I asked Mrs. Drysdale, the housekeeper who looked after her, if she had mentioned to her about my Mother's death. Mrs. Drysdale said "No."

When we entered Mrs. Harris's room, she came forward to greet us and said she was pleased to see us. We sat down without mentioning the fact that we had come for a séance, but just as if we had come to pay her a passing visit, my brother saying that when he heard she was in Glasgow he just wanted to come and shake hands with her.

After a few words of general conversation Mrs. Harris spoke to us as follows:

"You seem to bring an atmosphere of sorrow with you today." Then she paused. "Someone has passed on within the past week. A lady, small, stooping, old. I should say about eighty years of age. Very closely connected with you. Nellie brings her with her." (10)

I now summarise what Mrs. Harris had still to say, but she had much more to tell us when the time had arrived for her to go downstairs and take the service in the church. So she said: "Come back after the church service, and we may be able to get more through." I mention this because, with the sitting I had with Mrs. Abbot in London, a few days later, reference was made to two separate occasions on which my Mother had communicated, which was correct. Mrs. Harris had no opportunity to inquire about my Mother as she came downstairs along with me and, immediately she left the platform she joined me and my brother and we returned to her room with her. What was said at both these sittings is now incorporated hereunder, as if it had all occurred at the same time.

Mrs. Harris passed into trance and her controlling spirit spoke as follows: "The lady had no feeling of surprise when she passed over, only a feeling of great joy to touch dear Robert's hand." (1)

Mrs. Harris's control then referred to Robert (my Father) meeting her when she passed over and also "an old gentleman who had passed on recently". "This old gentleman welcomed her, but was now looking after someone else" (Annie, his sister, just died). "The lady gives her name as Margaret, and Nellie" (my brother's deceased wife) "says: 'Just as I came and brought the old gentleman in Glasgow and then in London, so shall I bring your Mother to you in London as I have brought her this morning.'" (6)

(This reference is to Nellie bringing my uncle to Glasgow the day before his funeral to speak to John and then, on a later occasion, to speak to John in London.)

"The lady mentions Mary and Elizabeth. She sends them both her love and gratitude. She has mentioned them in her Will, giving them recognition. It is a money recognition." "I always like to pay my debts," she says. "I have tried to repay them for all their kindness to me." Her last conscious remembrance on earth was Mary and Elizabeth standing beside her. "Elizabeth stroked my hand and face with her hand. She was alone with me at the time." (9)

I then asked: "Have you seen your old school friend?" and the reply was: "Yes, Annie, big woman. She would nearly fill the doorway." (2)

"Your Mother speaks of a red rose which was placed on her robe in her coffin on her breast." She says: "Red is my favourite colour, but why did you not put the rose in my hand?" (5)

"Your Mother had very small hands and feet; she was proud of her small feet, she took size twos in shoes." (4)

The medium went on: "Arthur's daughter, your Mother tells me, is young and tall, but was not present at your Mother's passing, as she was away from home at the time." (5)

"Your Mother mentions John's boys, one of them, who is seventeen, is tall, the other, Arthur—not this Arthur" (pointing to me)—"I am more concerned about. Carry out what she advises and push him forward." (5)

"Your Mother mentions various small gifts she has left for people with cards attached bearing messages and names. Arthur's daughter's gift is a necklace." (4)

"Your Mother asks me to tell you she tried to retain consciousness till you, Arthur, and Gertrude arrived. You rushed up from a long distance. She did not succeed in remaining conscious, but so long as she was conscious she kept thinking of them coming." (4)

The medium's control then spoke to John, saying that he had recently had his birthday, but that he had not yet bought his Mother's present. He had first told her he would not buy a book, and then had changed his mind and decided to buy one. (4)

"She tells me," the control went on, "that John's books are becoming numerous and that his library is becoming like Nellie's handkerchiefs. Then she goes on to say that John put a piece of paper in his waistcoat pocket and that had reference to this book." (5)

(The reference to Nellie's handkerchiefs was good, because Nellie, when she was ill, bought so many handkerchiefs at one time that there was a joke about it. As to John putting a piece of paper in his waistcoat pocket, he had done so that morning to remind him to order the book at the Church Bookstall.)

"Your Mother mentions something in her bedroom with a small single drawer in it containing papers which will interest you both." When we said we did not know of such a thing, she mentioned a bunch of keys and we said we did not know anything about this bunch of keys. (5)

(When we returned home we looked round her room and saw her dressing-case, which was a mahogany box about 18 inches by 18 inches. We could not open it as it was locked, and we asked for the key. This was on a bunch of keys. The dressing-case was opened, and after examining the inside we found a spring which released a single drawer in which we found quite a number of papers of interest. If we had not been told about this drawer it is unlikely we would ever have found these papers.)

The medium then referred to my Mother having pain in her stomach and weakness of her heart, also to sickness. She referred also to her having weak knees. She then referred to one eye being very troublesome: "Not blind, you know, but sore and uncomfortable." She goes like this." (The medium's hand went up to her eye, as my Mother was continually doing when her eye was troublesome, her right finger going round her eye.) (8)

"Your Mother died of something wrong here." (The medium put her hand to her stomach.) "Your Father died of something here." (She put her hand on her appendix.) "Your Mother has left three grown-up people and three children." (Myself, my brother, my wife, my daughter and John's two sons.) (4)

"Your Mother was very fond of her Bible, and a little old village church with a bell in a small pointed steeple. She could hear the bell ringing from her home." (5)

"Your Mother loved the hills but she now sees hills like those she could see from her home." (2)

"Your Mother has met Dr. Lamond; she hardly

recognised him as he is looking so much younger than when she saw him last." (2)

"Your Mother refers to a picture of Nellie on the piano in a room with a high ceiling with a pattern round it. It is a coloured picture." (5)

"Your Mother said that during the recent church service Arthur moved up to the end of the pew, and she came and sat beside him." (1)

(This is correct about me moving up to the end of the pew, but, when I did do so, the medium was in trance on the platform and could not have seen me. In any case, I was sitting far back in the church. This was said at the sitting we had after the service.)

All that was said in the sitting we had after the church service occurred with the medium in trance. Mrs. Harris, just before we left her, when saying good-bye, mentioned that before we arrived she had received a message which she had not understood. When she was dressing that morning, Nellie had appeared to her and said that Arthur and John were coming to see her that morning. She did not know who Arthur and John were, but she mentioned this message to us as a matter of interest.

Everything reported above is quite applicable to my Mother and the other people mentioned. Ninety-six facts were given which the medium could not have known. Not one single statement was incorrect or even doubtful.

SITTING WITH MRS. ABBOT IN LONDON ON 12TH FEBRUARY, 1936

On the above date I had a sitting with Mrs. Abbot in a private room at The London Spiritualist Alliance.

Mrs. Abbot went into trance quickly and her control stated that "an elderly lady was present, from seventy-five to eighty years, belonging to me. She had recently passed over." (3)

"Amongst those who were waiting for her was a clergyman uncle, who, when on earth, thought Spiritualism was the work of the Devil. He was an ardent minister, and used to wear a red hood, but he has now given up the foolish ideas which he preached." (4)

"Your Father and Mother are both in the spirit world, and they send you their love. All is well with your Mother. This is not the first time she has come back to you, as she came back on two occasions before, but the first time she could not get through well; the second time, she got through what she wanted quite well." (4)

"Your Mother learned a lot about the after-life from you (Arthur) before dying. She feels much younger now. She has met Nellie. Your Father is very happy having her with him. Your Father can never thank you enough for all you did for your Mother. It will be repaid in the years to come. You have many years in front of you, and he is glad that people look up to you. He approves of your books." (3)

"Nellie's Mother is also here but finds it very difficult to understand the new conditions. She will take a long time to understand them, as she was so attached to earth and the things of the earth." (2)

"For a long time your Mother was against your views and did not believe in what you believed. Though she was very proud of her two sons, yet she was so tied down to what she was taught in childhood that she could not realise that things could be different from what she had then been taught. She feels very humble and subdued now and is not so opinionative as she was on earth." (5)

"Your Mother saw Nellie just before she passed over. Your Father was also waiting for her. When she got over here your Father said to her: 'What do you think of all this?', to which she replied: 'I suppose I am dead, but I never felt like dying.' Your Father replied: 'You were never dead and you never will be dead.' Your Father put her to bed to rest when she got here."

"For some weeks before she died her mind was very forgetful. She was losing a grip on earth life. She just slept away quite peacefully. When she arrived here she was not so surprised as many other people are, because of what you had told her. For some years before passing her legs were bad, but now she feels quite young again, and her great freedom of movement is one of the things that impresses her most in her new life. She has now a much nicer garden than she had in her own home." (6)

Then reference was made to the two boys. "They are Ian's sons." (Ian is Gaelic for John, and is his home name.) "One was named Arthur, but his name had been changed, owing to the confusion with you, to a name connected with the family. Your Mother objected to the change at first, but now thinks it was a good idea to change the name." (6)

Then reference was made to her furniture, and "she hoped that the big furniture would not be sold." (1). (This was her wish on earth.)

Reference was next made to old family papers and to old family photographs. "They are not old rubbish and, though you are not interested in them, you should keep them." (3). (Correct. She knew I was not specially interested in these, and she had made this remark, in these words, when on earth, to me.)

"Her Father," she said, "was like you in looks. He would push in where angels feared to tread. Very stern and at times she was in awe of him, but looked up to him, as no one could help doing so. She is very fond of him." (7)

She then referred to a visit of recent years to Bournemouth which I had forgotten, and said so, but she said this was correct, and I now remember that a few years before she died, my wife and I did stay with her at an hotel in Bournemouth for a few days. (1)

"Your Mother is very grateful to Nellie for her kindness to her since she arrived, and for helping her to come back and speak to you. She never could have imagined that Nellie could have been of such help. She has just been like a nurse. Your Mother was not always too nice to Nellie, and used to blame Ian for spoiling her, but will not do so again, as Nellie is well worthy of it. Nellie's Mother used not to be very nice with her either. Your Mother is also very grateful to Gertrude (my wife) for all her kindness to her, which she much appreciated." (6)

She then referred to the pretty nurse who looked after her. She said she liked her very much indeed. She also liked drinking the powdered stuff just before passing, as it made her mouth feel clean and relieved discomfort. (4)

I then asked my Mother what G.W.G. stood for.

"The control stated that she was laughing, and that, though she could not explain what the initials stood for, yet she was not that now. She was having to lie low and not say too much, as she felt somewhat subdued after all the opinions she had given on earth. She said she was not a G.W.G. any longer." (5). (Correct. G.W.G. stood for "Great Wee Girl" which we called her when she became opinionative.)

"Your Mother was very autocratic, yet homely. She did not like to be pushed on one side, but liked to feel she was someone in the home. Her legs were rather bad towards the end, but now she can walk and feels bright and fresh. She so loved her country place and her garden, but now she is in a place where there is no fog and dullness. Three months before her passing her sight became bad, but she can now see clearly and further than before." (6)

"She brings a stick and says she has now no need for a stick. This is symbolic of her religious outlook. What you told her about her religion was true. When she awoke on the other side she saw a bright light which she thought was Christ, but it was your Father. It will be some time before she understands all you told her, but her outlook is much brighter now than it has ever been." (2)

"She is glad Ian's two boys are getting on so well and she wants you to look after the maid who took such care of her. Mary had to put up with so much from her and was always so gentle and patient. Don't cast her aside but keep her in the family." (7)

Mrs. Abbot's control then said he would like Nellie to control the medium herself. Nellie then spoke to me, calling me Arthur throughout. She put her hand (the medium's hand) out, and shook hands with me. She started off by saying: "Your Mother is all right." She said: "I just wish my own Mother had a clearer outlook on things, but unfortunately she was kept on the astral plane because of her egotism, her love of subservience, and having people always bowing down to her and loving to be the centre of everything." (5)

"Your Father asked me to tell you that if you go to Sloan he will try and get your Mother to speak to you by the direct voice." Nellie then said: "I would like my darling Ian to go with you to Sloan so that I can speak to him also." (2)

Nellie continued: "Your Mother was conscious almost to the last and passed over without any suffering, and quite naturally. Your Mother is very much more willing to learn about her new life than is my Mother. It is sad for me not to be able to be with her more as she cannot rise to the plane in which we live, but this will come some day." (1)

In reply to a question, Nellie said: "Yes, we are living just above you and can come to you instantly. We have very bright diffused light which is very much more pleasant than the light from your sun, as it is not so glaring."

Then she referred to Jack, who, "owing to his contrition and the shame he felt for what he had done, had risen to be with the rest of them. He was never bad at heart, in fact he was a very warm-hearted and kind-hearted man. Until he felt shame and remorse he could not rise to where we are, but whenever that came on him, and he saw his mistakes, he was able to mix with us. He certainly did very odd things which seemed to be selfish, but not really selfishness. He was quite a good-hearted man." (7)

Then she referred to her Father, who was with her, and said: "The love of money and earth's goods had not spoiled him the way it had spoiled my Mother." (2)

Nellie then said: "Your Mother would have to unlearn all her past religious ideas, but she would soon do that under your Father's guidance."

Nellie then spoke about the conditions over there, emphasising that their world was very much like ours. She said that when she arrived first of all she saw a beautiful little waterfall and went and put her hand under the water. When she pulled her hand away it was quite dry and she did not feel the water. When she bathes in their sea she gets all the pleasure and exhilaration of bathing but is never wet, and comes out of the water quite dry.

In reply to a question, she confirmed what I have already been told, that to come back to earth they come through their own surface, but it was just a question of tuning in to the vibrations of the different surface levels. Yes, they had towns and villages and everything was very beautiful and they never had any darkness.

The sitting lasted for an hour and a half. When Mrs. Abbot came out of trance I asked her if she knew my brother, and she said "No." She recognised me because she had seen me going about the London Spiritualist Alliance building, but that she never, to her knowledge, had met my brother, which confirms what my brother had told me that Mrs. Abbot did not know him.

This being so, the information given is all the more interesting, especially the story about Nellie putting her hand under the waterfall, because Nellie told John the same story through another medium.

Mrs. Abbot said, after coming out of trance, that she was quite unaware that my Mother had recently passed on, and I do not see how she could have heard of it, or known about it, as, after the sitting, I mentioned it to one or two others in the London Spiritualist Alliance, who had not heard of it. It was mentioned only once in *The Times*, but, even if Mrs. Abbot had seen it, I do not see how she could have connected her name with me, in fact I am quite certain that she never knew my Mother had died.

The sitting was arranged by the Secretary of the International Institute for Psychical Research, but no name was given. That being so, Mrs. Abbot had no opportunity to make enquiries, and, when I arrived for the séance, I walked up to her room and found her waiting. She said she had an appointment with someone at two o'clock, but she did not know who it was, and I told her I was the person for whom the appointment was made.

Everything stated above is correct and applicable to my Mother and the others mentioned. Ninety-two facts were given at this séance, none of which the medium could have known. So, if we add together the facts given at the two sittings, we find ninety-six facts given at the sitting on 9th February, 1936, and ninety-two facts given at the sitting on 12th February, 1936, making one hundred and eighty-eight in all.

Not one of the statements made was incorrect or even doubtful.

The subjects discussed in this book are more fully considered in *The Rock of Truth*, *The Unfolding Universe* and *Looking Back*.

Mr. Findlay's book, *Where Two Worlds Meet*, records many verbatim conversations between this world and the next in the presence of John Sloan. Hundreds of different voices from the other world spoke by means of the Direct Voice, Mr. Sloan remaining normal and taking part in the conversation. Everything said on both sides was taken down at the time by an expert stenographer and retyped immediately.

This book is one of the most convincing records in existence that life continues after death. Besides giving much interesting information about the other world and how they live there, we are made to realise how interested our friends are still in us, and how anxious they are to speak to us and tell us that they still live.

Their affection for us is as great as when they were on earth. Vivid descriptions are given of the other world, how they live, where they live, what they think, besides much evidence of their surviving personalities.